NAVIGATING
LOSS

NAVIGATING
LOSS

WISDOM AND SELF-CARE FOR TIMES OF GRIEF AND THE CHALLENGES OF LIFE

HEATHER STANG

CICO BOOKS
LONDON NEW YORK

IN HONOR OF MARY THERESA DECKER
1964–2024

Published in 2024 by CICO Books
An imprint of Ryland Peters & Small Ltd
20–21 Jockey's Fields   341 E 116th St
London WC1R 4BW   New York, NY 10029

www.rylandpeters.com

10 9 8 7 6 5 4 3 2 1

A CIP catalog record for this book is available from the Library of Congress and the
British Library.

ISBN: 978-1-80065-379-5

Printed in China

Editor: Emma Hill
Illustrator: Camila Gray
Commissioning editor: Kristine Pidkameny
Senior designer: Emily Breen
Art director: Sally Powell
Creative director: Leslie Harrington
Head of production: Patricia Harrington
Publishing manager: Carmel Edmonds

CONTENTS

TABLE OF PRACTICES

PROLOGUE

A JOURNEY OF LOSS
AND HEALING

EVERYONE'S LOSS MATTERS

When my new husband and I were pronounced man and wife on the Sanibel Island beach, dolphins jumped out of the water. I am not making this up. It was a gift. A blessing. A sign, for sure, that the universe sanctioned our marriage.

Except, as you can imagine from the subject of this book, it wasn't. Ten years later, we would divorce. It turns out that our so-called wedding dolphins were just doing basic dolphin things.

Because I love math, and statistics in particular, the fact that our marriage ended is not surprising. If I am honest with myself, the moment my future husband proposed, I felt not joy, but deep and foreboding dread. And yet, I said yes.

Growing up, I unconsciously learned that acting on instinct was unsafe; doing so would lead to being labeled difficult, unreasonable, or my favorite, histrionic. I was conditioned to do the opposite of what I thought was right. Saying yes when my body said no was a habit that had been deeply ingrained in me since my childhood.

This is why I ignored the alarm bells going off in my body the night he proposed. Instead, I focused on the attractive man holding the ring, asking me to be his wife, while floating on a gondola in Las Vegas, serenaded by a gondolier whose name tag said "Figaro." I entered into a dreamlike state—one in which I could not say no.

So, I said yes to the fantasy. To the dream of happily ever after, of mattering to someone, of being able to love fully and to be fully loved. And on a deep unconscious level, the goal of the fantasy was to prove my father wrong. I wanted to show that I could be loved.

Ever since I can remember, I believed no man would ever want me, because this is what was demonstrated in both the words and actions of my father. I bought into the idea that I was too aggressive, too independent, too weird. When I was left with a scar on my knee from a bike accident, my father offered to take me for plastic surgery. Generous on the surface, perhaps, but followed with "You need to get that fixed because when you are older, men will walk by you on the beach and not give you a second glance." I am not sure what made my thirteen-year-old self more frightened: the idea of surgery, foreshadowed rejection, or the fact that my father could be so hurtful.

When my fiancé and I returned home from Las Vegas, I slid into the role of happy bride-to-be with an outward ease masking inner anxiety. To be fair, I did love him. I wanted him to be my "ride or die"—my partner, best friend, and confidant. Once married, I did my best to keep the peace, denying the fear triggered by broken promises, gaslighting, and the financial infidelity that years later resulted in a tax lien on our house and my working three jobs to support an unsustainable lifestyle. I couldn't imagine leaving, both because I loved my husband and because I wanted to prove my father wrong.

It took a particularly chaotic visit from my dad for me to realize that I wasn't the whole problem. I finally saw clearly what my therapist had been telling me for years; that I was in a codependent relationship with, well, pretty much everybody. For two years my dad and I tried to repair our relationship, but finally I realized that we were just not healthy for one another.

"Cutting yourself off from a parent is, psychologically, a very big deal," my therapist told me during a two-hour session, when I had read my dad's and my letters back-to-back in chronological order. "Expect to grieve." I asked my father for no contact, and grieve I did.

While deeply painful, and not something I entered into lightly, letting go of my paternal baggage created a healing space in my life. Once I dropped the story of not being worthy, wanted, or cherished, I was able to investigate the deep fissures in my marriage. And just as I had with my dad's and my relationship, I tried to save Us. I wanted to save Us. However, as you already know, that relationship ended, too. More grief.

To many, my story may not seem particularly horrific. And that's kind of the point. That's the reason I'm sharing it. The types of losses I experienced— divorce, parental estrangement, identity, financial hardship, my home, stability, childhood innocence, betrayal, and the dream I had for how my life would unfold—are so common that they are often invisible not only to others, but to ourselves. Ubiquity, however, does not make any of these losses less painful.

My privilege is not lost on me. I know without a doubt that I have access to resources for navigating loss that many people in the world do not. All I can do is try to share what I've learned in my personal healing. My goal is to give life to my gratitude by acting from a place of service, reverence, and compassion to reduce suffering.

Everyone's loss matters. Everyone's pain matters. Everyone includes you. As you learn how to cope with the loss that led you to pick up this book, know that it is natural for present losses to intensify the grief of a previous loss.

Together, we will peel back the layers of this very human existence to get to what remains: your ability to do more than just survive. Whether you are learning how to live fully with your loss once more—or for the first time—you will learn to craft a future that resonates with who you want to be. Maybe this doesn't feel possible right now, but one step at a time, you will arrive.

I am not saying that grief is a gift, though I do think it can be an invitation. You are in a place you do not want to be, otherwise you wouldn't have picked up this book. What wouldn't we trade to have things back to how we wanted them to be? But here we are, you and I and our grief. This book is my invitation to you to mindfully engage with the meaning you have for both what you've lost and what you have left.

As you walk with me on this healing journey, you will learn that joy and sorrow can coexist. While all beginnings have an end, those endings can lead to a new beginning. And as unwelcome as change is, the most significant growth, compassion, and meaning often blooms from our deepest pain. You will start to live again, and, eventually, create the life you want.

While this book is an inanimate object, please know that there is a real human on the other side of these words, wishing that you didn't have to suffer, and I am willing to give you everything I know to help you navigate loss in the healthiest way possible.

Let's begin the journey of finding the light in the darkness together.

With loving kindness,

Heather Stang

INTRODUCTION

WHAT IS LOSS?

A NEW PERSPECTIVE ON GRIEF

When I was earning my master's degree in thanatology—the study of death, dying, and bereavement—I was taught that the word "grief" should be used only when discussing the "uncontrollable reaction" to the death of a living being. "Loss" was a more fluid term, general enough to describe both death and non-death loss alike. This distinction hinged on the concept of permanence. My teachers reasoned that you can always buy a new house, get a new job, find another partner, or even remarry a person you divorced, whereas death is irreversible. If any of this made you bristle, read on.

My perspective was challenged while attending the 2019 Association of Death Education and Counseling (ADEC) annual conference. Dr Darcy Harris, Professor and Thanatology Department faculty member at King's University College in London, Canada, delivered a keynote advocating for more sensitivity toward non-death losses within our field. Harris' interest in this subject began when researching couples going through infertility treatment.

She observed that even though the loss the couples were experiencing was the end of a dream rather than the end of a life, the language they used to describe their pain was the same language used by people grieving a physical death. This inspired her to research the intersection of non-death loss and grief theory, leading to insightful books including *Counting Our Losses: Reflecting on Change, Loss, and Transition in Everyday Life* (2011) and *Non-Death Loss and Grief: Context and Clinical Implications* (2020). Harris' work advanced the application of grief therapies when supporting clients through non-death loss; it also serves as the foundation of this book.

The idea of opening the definition of grief up to include death *and* non-death loss was unsettling to me for personal and professional reasons. In my own narrative of love and loss, my deepest grief began with the *deaths* of my uncle, my stepfather, and our family dog Brandy. From a professional standpoint, my resistance stemmed from respect for my beloved thanatology professors, a deep desire to uphold their teachings, and the fact that, back then, I rarely questioned anyone in a position of authority.

I do not remember the exact words Dr Harris spoke in her keynote on Non-Death Loss and Grief, but I will never forget how I felt when she explained that adjusting to non-death losses could be just as unmooring as a death-related loss. This is because the impact of loss is shaped by individual circumstances. I remember sitting up straight, eyes wide, and tilting my head as tears filled my eyes and a deep sense of bittersweet understanding washed over my body. It was at that moment that I realized that my narrow view of grief had minimized my own very significant non-death loss: the estranged relationship with my father.

Harris defines loss as "An experience where there is a change in circumstance, perception, or experience where it would be impossible to return to the way things were before."[1] She likens it to a pane of glass that has shattered; while the pieces can be reassembled and glued back together, the original, unaltered pane will never be restored to its former state. This interpretation led me to an internal reckoning. If you'll recall, the primary argument for separating non-death losses from bereavement was the concept of permanence. But I now agree that the idea that death is the *only* permanent loss is erroneous. My father may still be alive, but the impact of our estrangement is irreversible. Even if we did reconcile, like the shattered glass, I am forever changed.

I can now hold space for both these truths: death is painful, disruptive, disorienting, and lasting—*and* non-death loss can be these things, too. When it comes to loss, we can care instead of compare. The hardest loss for any of us is the one we are experiencing.

This book is for *all* those hardest losses. The deaths, the divorces, the dreams, the routines, the autonomy, the careers, the stability, the identities, the wellness, the safety, and any and everything else that has left you unmoored. Living with a chronic illness, parenting a child with a disability, adjusting to the ongoing impact of a life-altering injury, or facing the perpetual uncertainty brought on by a loved one's mental health obstacles or addiction are just some of the nonfinite losses that, for some, are just as hard as a death.

Death itself can bring with it many non-death losses—the future you planned that will never come to pass, the sense of security that vanished, or the circle of friends or family relationships that became strained. These secondary losses may not be as visible but are no less deeply felt and deserve their own space and recognition. That recognition is what you will find in these pages. If you're looking for a deeper exploration of death-related loss specifically, you will find it in my first book, *Living with Grief: Mindful Meditations and Self-care Strategies for Navigating Loss*.

MIA'S STORY:
LIFE'S INEVITABLE CHANGES AND LOSSES

In early March 2020, Mia attended a continuing education program on infectious diseases for massage therapists. Little did she know that a global pandemic was just weeks away. She simply respected the instructor and wanted to earn her required continuing education credits. Mia was surprised to reunite with classmates she met in her massage therapy program back in 1996. It had been years since they graduated, and life had taken them all in different directions.

As they caught up, Mia learned that most of her former classmates were facing tough times. Their businesses were struggling, and many were navigating either health or relationship issues, sometimes both. This was not only true for her close peers; it seemed to be a common theme with the massage therapists who had traveled from different states to attend the class.

Unlike her peers, Mia's career was thriving. She had built a successful massage therapy business over her 24 years in practice, and was always booked months in advance. Her personal life was equally fulfilling with her significant other, Teddy. Despite a massive heart attack in 2006, Teddy defied the odds, living well beyond the two-year prognosis doctors predicted without a heart transplant. Mia also navigated her own health challenges, including a hip replacement and surgeries for a salivary gland stone and basal cell cancer.

Mia's stable world began to crumble just one week after the infectious disease class, as COVID-19 turned into a pandemic and state mandates forced her to close her business for one and a half years. In an effort to generate income, Mia launched an online wellness summit, tapping into her earlier skills as a communication consultant and video producer. Despite her talent, fear and uncertainty shadowed her every step. With no income, and hesitant to tap into Social Security at the age of 64, the financial pressure mounted.

"My entire world had changed almost overnight. I felt like I had lost my identity, my purpose, my people, and my health. I was so grateful to have Teddy. He became my everything." But concern for Teddy's health grew, and socially, Mia felt isolated. All the years working six days a week, 12 hours a day had left little room for friendships beyond Teddy and her clientele. The physical distancing didn't help her feeling of isolation. Even once the restrictions were lifted, Mia and Teddy continued to isolate due to their individual health concerns.

Then her worst fear came true. Teddy died—not from COVID-19—but from his long-standing heart condition. In losing him, Mia felt the ground beneath her give way. She lost her partner, her emotional anchor, and with him, a big part of her world.

It was around this time that I met Mia, who joined my online grief support program, Awaken. As she shared her story with me, my heart felt like lead. The scope of loss she carried was immense—almost too much for one person to endure. Yet, as I listened, I knew her experience mirrored a global narrative of loss that many were experiencing. The pandemic not only claimed lives, but the everyday normalcy, security, and connections we once took for granted.

While Teddy's death was the focal point of her grief, Mia's journey underscored the need to recognize and address the multitude of losses that had silently piled up in her life. I trusted, as I always have, that the work we would do together would help her find her footing once more.

Mia's story serves as a poignant reminder that loss extends far beyond the death of loved ones. When anything we hold dear is taken away—our people, our pets, our livelihood, our health, our security—it challenges our sense of stability and identity. Mia's journey, while uniquely hers, offers valuable insights into the collective experience of navigating life's inevitable changes and uncertainties. Just like her, so many people lost so much during the pandemic that it seemed the whole world succumbed to a form of global compassion fatigue. It validated what I realized during Dr Harris' 2019 keynote. It isn't a question of whether a death or non-death loss is harder, grief in any form is disorienting, painful, and requires us to adapt, because we cannot return to how things were before.

RENOVATING YOUR ASSUMPTIVE WORLD

Whether your loss is one big event, a series of misfortunes, or a million tiny stones piling up until you feel crushed under their weight, the act of reading this book means you have hope; hope means you are one step closer to digging your way out of the rubble. Loss has a way of changing your internal geography, rendering the landscape you once knew unfamiliar or even unrecognizable.

Grief upends your assumptive world—the unique lens through which you see your life—a perception shaped by your individual upbringing, beliefs, and experiences. It includes how you appraise other people and their intentions, how you believe the world should work, and how you perceive yourself. Your assumptive world informs your sense of safety and your narratives about the past, present, and future. This perspective is so ingrained in your psyche that you might not even recognize it is there—until it is challenged by loss and/or trauma.[2]

Like Mia, your loss may feel like it has completely demolished everything you hold dear, destroyed the ground beneath your feet. But you will learn how to adjust to the changes, and even go beyond mere survival. The tools in this book will help you craft a solid foundation for an even more resilient structure, just like rebuilding a home damaged by high-speed wind and rain with new hurricane-resistant materials. As with any devastating storm, loss leaves us with no other choice other than to pick up the toolbox and get to work.

And, just as restoring a house combines old materials with new, rebuilding your assumptive world will include a mix of established and fresh points of view. When it comes to grief, journaling, movement, meditation, and ritual will be your wood, brick, insulation, and drywall. These time-tested tools will not only help you cope with this season of loss, but will help you savor what remains, and weather whatever the future brings.

If you've ever worked with a contractor, you'll know that construction projects often take longer than the time that was originally estimated. Grief is no different. Recalibrating your existential view will include unexpected delays and setbacks. Just because progress is not linear does not mean it is not happening. So, if you are wondering how long will this take, my answer is that I don't know—but it will happen. What I do know is that if you trust the process and use the practices in this book, you will be able to rebuild a world you want to live in again—one brick at a time.

You wouldn't want to live in a structure where corners were cut during construction to speed up your move-in date. Nor should you rush the process of rebuilding your assumptive world, as this can lead to structural weaknesses that may plague you down the road. Grief work is not a quick fix; it is an adaptation to the natural rhythms of loss, a period of trial-and-error while you learn how to take care of the one who is grieving—you. If you honor your feelings, recognize that progress comes in waves, and practice self-kindness and patience, you will indeed create a new sturdy, sustainable, assumptive world—one that is safe for you to live in.

LEARNING HOW TO GRIEVE

For over 20 years I have witnessed clients transition from deep grief to living fully, but this is not to say it is a welcome task. No one chooses the heartache of loss. And unfortunately, only you can show up for you 100% of the time. Even our closest allies may not always be able to show up for us. Sometimes the person that would normally help you through is the one you are now estranged from, or they are coping with their own loss, or they are the one who died. The only person that can give you the care and support you need anytime, day or night, is you.

I have a love-hate relationship with this truth. There is a part of me that wishes that we could all rely on someone other than ourselves to support us consistently, without fail. That same part of me wants to kick and scream and throw a temper tantrum when I realize that the only person who can truly take care of me is *me*. It simply doesn't seem fair. But it is reality. Learning how to tend to yourself in this way is the greatest skill you will ever cultivate, because it teaches you how to meet your own needs. I am grateful that I've learned how to companion myself through tough times, and I hope you find the same to be true. I am always with me, just as you are always with you.

If this makes you want to run in the other direction, I understand. But this will not reduce your suffering. What will help is choosing to learn how to grieve. Mary-Francis O'Connor, grief researcher, neuroscientist, and author of *The Grieving Brain: The Surprising Science of How We Learn from Love and Loss*, writes, "Because learning is something we do our whole lives, seeing grieving as a type of learning may make it feel more familiar and understandable and give us the patience to allow this remarkable process to unfold." From how to cope with a wide range of emotions to exploring who you were and who you want to be now, grieving is fundamentally about learning.

Savor this: you are actively choosing to engage in this learning by reading these words. I do not know you or the intimate details of your story, but I do know something very important about you; if you are holding this book, it is because you are going through an incredibly tough time. I also know that, because you opened this book, there is a part of you that has hope, and there is a part of you that is ready to learn.

HOW TO GET THE MOST OUT OF THIS BOOK

Within these pages you will find a framework to navigate all forms of loss. Most chapters include a real-world story from myself or my clients, with names and identifying details altered for confidentiality unless otherwise requested. I have tried my best to offer a variety of loss narratives; however, whether or not yours is represented, if you focus on the common themes of loss and adaptation you will get something out of each one. Similarly, while not every practice, theory, or type of grief will apply to your situation, choose what works for you and do not try to force anything that does not resonate.

This book is organized into three types of content:

- Chapters 1 and 2 focus on the foundations of grief and loss, and help you normalize what likely feels like an extremely abnormal experience.

- Chapters 3–9 give you the practical tools to cope with the pain of loss, adapt to the myriad of changes, and, while it may seem impossible right now, build a life that you want to live.

- Chapters 10–12 address the external elements of loss, including getting support for yourself, offering support to others, and coping with global loss and devastation.

While I encourage you to read through the chapters and their practices in order, if you are struggling with a particular challenge and want to skip ahead, trust your instincts.

The practices in this book will help you put theory into action, so you apply what you have read within your daily life to create change. I often compare reading a self-help book to a cookbook; reading it alone will not create a delicious meal. You have to shop, gather your tools, prepare the ingredients, and then let it simmer. So please take your time with each chapter and practice. While you may be tempted to rush through them in an effort to ease your pain more quickly, metabolizing the information and embodying each practice will have long-term benefits that are worth savoring.

All that being said, it does not take long for you to start feeling a shift. Just like munching on a delicious carrot while you are chopping vegetables for a stew, many of my clients report that even a little bit of practice is helpful. It gives you hope and control, and your whole being enjoys benefits from the experience itself.

PREPARING YOUR SPACE

One of the most helpful things you can do for yourself is to dedicate a practice space in your home. This could be a whole room, or a quiet corner with a comfortable chair, calm music, and perhaps even aromatherapy to enhance your sense of comfort and focus. Many find comfort in having tactile objects such as soft blankets, pillows, and even stuffed animals close by, symbolizing self-compassion and support.

While the yoga practices in this book are gentle and do not require a yoga mat, you will want to at least place one or more blankets under you on the floor for cushioning if you engage in the somatic yoga therapy exercises (see Chapter 4).

JOURNALING

Last, but certainly not least, is your journal. There are many benefits to keeping track of your experience, and most chapters have guided prompts. I want to stress that this is very different from writing in school, and you do not need to be good at it to take part. In fact, no one will be reading it, grading it, or marking it up in red ink.

Your journal may be as simple as a spiral-bound notebook, which you can write in with a reliable pen or pencil. This is my favorite choice, because writing by hand involves more attention and focus, resulting in a more embodied and mindful experience. It also reduces distractions and takes most of us out of our usual default of being connected to a screen. But if you prefer, you can go digital and use a word processing program or one of the many journaling apps now available. Even voice-to-text or voice recordings can work, but while audio recordings can capture the emotion of the moment, they may be more challenging to review later.

The benefits to journaling through loss are many. First, there is the physical act of moving what is inside your head to outside of your body. This externalization helps you examine your thoughts from a different perspective. Second, writing down your experiences both reveals and reinforces insights and revelations. Third, this written record will be invaluable when you read back through it months or years down the road, and see just how much you have learned and changed along the way. Finally, your journal is like a love letter to yourself. In it you speak your truth and have the freedom to be your authentic self. If you fall in love with journaling, and want more prompts, please seek out my guided journal, *From Grief to Peace*.

SOURCES OF KNOWLEDGE

Finally, I want to acknowledge that while I have compiled these stories and practices into this volume, they are deeply rooted in the timeless wisdom of Buddhist and Hindu traditions, as well as in the fields of psychology and thanatology. I do not claim ownership over these rich legacies but express deep gratitude to the teachers, yogis, sages, monks, and researchers who have created, preserved, and shared these insights. You, too, are an expert on your own journey, as your inner voice holds invaluable wisdom. In that sense, you are a teacher as well. May their guidance, along with your inner wisdom, inspire you on your journey, and may you find their teachings as precious and transformative as I do.

CHAPTER 1

THE ROCKY TERRAIN OF UNACKNOWLEDGED LOSS

FINDING SUPPORT WHEN YOUR GRIEF IS DISMISSED

Imagine hiking up a steep slope through a dense, unfamiliar forest, carrying a heavy backpack. A group of hikers descend past you, smiling and oblivious to your struggle. Shortly after, another group passes by. They can tell you are straining with every step, but instead of offering help, they quicken their pace to move by as fast as possible. Finally, a group of well-outfitted, athletic types sprint by, mumbling under their breath that maybe you should be better prepared the next time you try to climb such a difficult mountain. Their message is painfully clear: you don't have the right to be here.

When your grief is unseen, ignored, or belittled, it stings. In those moments, it helps to turn to a well-meaning soul who cares enough to share a moment of silence, hug you when you need it, or offer just the right words at the right time. Someone who understands that there is no one right way to do this, and gives you the dignity to grieve how you need to, and at your own pace. But unfortunately, the saying that grief rewrites your address book is often true; it's a startling realization when familiar sources of support fall short of providing the comfort you desperately seek in times of loss.

Even the people closest to you, especially those who are struggling with the same emotional load as you, may not have the bandwidth to meet your needs. A skilled grief therapist or loss support group can help validate your feelings, teach you strategies to cope with your pain, and guide you through adapting to life after loss while fostering resilience. In Chapters 3–9, I'll share some of my favorite techniques that I offer in my online grief support group, Awaken. I also want to emphasize my faith in the transformative power of peer support groups. With proper guidance and facilitation, what may initially feel like a gathering of strangers soon evolves into a circle of compassionate friends, each member supporting the other through their journey of grief and healing.

You may also find this kind of magic in surprising places. I recently attended a machine knitting group (a rare vintage form of crafting), where during the bits of small talk a few people shared the hardships they were facing. One woman was widowed, another a bereaved mother, a few going through a divorce. Each person was acknowledged and comforted, asked questions, and not shut down. No one showed up for a grief group, and yet everyone walked away feeling seen and heard. This is humanity at its best.

Unfortunately, not everyone is this kind. Like our hiker from earlier in the chapter, the people in your life will exhibit a range of reactions: some supportive, others indifferent or even harshly dismissive. Without supportive people in your life, it is easy to feel isolated, stuck, and devoid of hope. But I want to encourage you to seek out individuals and groups that make you feel seen and comforted. I know this is extra hard when you're grieving, and ideally, the right people would just appear when we need them. But often, we have to advocate for ourselves to find the support we need.

DOMINIQUE'S STORY:
FINDING PEOPLE WHO UNDERSTAND YOU

Dominique and Richard's first date felt like something out of a dream—a marathon eight hours that left Dominique feeling seen and understood for the first time in a long while. But amid the whirlwind of new romance, there were faint signs that things were too good to be true. Richard was still legally married, a fact that gnawed at Dominique's conscience, even as she tried to rationalize her feelings away.

As the weeks turned into months, Dominique found herself increasingly involved in Richard's life. He was quick to declare her his girlfriend, bypassing any conversation about what they both wanted from the relationship. It was flattering, certainly, but so rushed it raised a red flag that fluttered at the edge of Dominique's awareness. He expressed his affection by showering her with gifts, but though she couldn't put her finger on it at the time, she was missing real emotional intimacy.

Dominique focused on supporting Richard through his divorce, often at the expense of her own needs. She fought beside him for custody of his dog, Jake, and went above and beyond to care for him during this tumultuous time. But as her efforts intensified, Richard's reciprocity began to wane. The balance shifted; the more Dominique gave, the less he seemed willing to return. When Dominique addressed this, Richard lashed out, his words cutting deep. He accused her of being selfish, of failing to appreciate the time they did spend together—a classic case of gaslighting that left Dominique questioning her own perceptions and feelings.

When Dominique's beloved cat died, it shook her to the core. "Maggie was my 'favorite' of my three fur children. She was the first cat that I lost, and my kitties mean everything to me, especially since I don't have kids and never got remarried after a divorce at a young age." Dominique was already grieving the death of her grandmother just one year earlier, and her cat was one of her strongest supports.

When she asked Richard to come over for comfort, he told her he was busy, and didn't show up until several days later. This broke her heart. When he finally showed up, he was anything but helpful, a stark reminder of the emotional chasm between them. Her grief, so palpable and all-consuming, was met with indifference, making her feel isolated in her sorrow.

"Richard said I was being very weak about my losses," Dominique shared during one of the Awaken grief support program meetings. "He feels the grief group is a constant reminder of my losses and is hurting me more than helping me." Hearing her story, the other members expressed their sadness over the lack of support. They were also baffled by his complete misunderstanding of how powerful it can be to share your feelings and experiences with others. The message that her feelings were valid empowered her to speak her truth to Richard, and she returned the next week still sad, but feeling more grounded in her truth.

The next week she shared, "I told him I thought it was really sad that he thinks tears are a sign of weakness. I explained that I feel people who can't tap into their emotions are truly the weak ones because they are too scared to face the challenges that emotions bring along. To hear these words from him was devastating." Ultimately, the realization that Richard could not offer the empathy and support she needed in her moment of vulnerability was a turning point. "Although I was still not in a good place, I was as ready as I could be for my next loss—the loss of 'the love of my life' and the dreams I had for our future. I could not bear to be treated this way anymore. I knew deep down I deserved more, even though it was going to hurt like hell."

DISENFRANCHISED GRIEF: THE SOCIAL LENS OF LOSS

Richard's inability to support Dominique was colored by his own aversion to vulnerability, and was likely influenced by accepted—but erroneous—social attitudes toward what counts as a loss. This disenfranchised grief is what happens when others fail to recognize the significance of a loss, either because the loss is not openly acknowledged, socially sanctioned, or publicly mourned. This lack of recognition and validation can have lasting negative effects on the grieving person, including feelings of isolation, loneliness, and misunderstanding.

Social expectations around grief can prevent other people from providing the support you urgently need, and may also discourage you from asking for it, lest you be met with shame or rejection. When support is denied, grief symptoms such as prolonged sadness, anxiety, depression, and somatic discomfort are often more pronounced. Dr Ken Doka, who coined this term, proposes five categories of disenfranchised grief, outlined below. As you read, you may find that any one loss may span several categories.

DISENFRANCHISED LOSSES

Losses that are perceived as inconsequential to others may hold a deep meaning for the grieving person: pet loss and intangible losses such as the death of a dream, safety, security, and losses that lack clarity or a defined end point. One common but no less painful loss is the "social death" that is experienced by dementia patients and their families, where they are physically present but psychologically disconnected. Alternatively, this can happen when someone is physically absent but remains a significant psychological presence, as with cases of brain death, missing persons, or adoption.

DISENFRANCHISED GRIEVERS

Particular groups of people, including the very young, the elderly, and individuals with developmental disabilities or neurodiverse ways of processing emotion often experience a lack of recognition or support during a loss. This can extend to anyone who doesn't fit the conventional expectations of "what a grieving person should look like." Such oversight not only marginalizes their experiences but also deprives them of the essential communal support needed to navigate the journey of grief.

DISENFRANCHISED RELATIONSHIPS

Grief support in Western cultures is often limited to the death of kin, to close immediate family or legally acknowledged partnerships. This overlooks the rich tapestry of relationships we have with mentors, colleagues, friends, classmates, or even online friends. Relationships that are often disenfranchised include ex-spouses, affair partners, LGBTQ+ relationships, and even long-term unmarried couples. This dismissal is all too often applied to non-death losses as well, including the end of friendships, non-married romantic relationships, living arrangements, or estrangements.

DISENFRANCHISED CIRCUMSTANCES

The method by which loss occurs may lead to stigmatization, often because the event is not socially acceptable, or is perceived as either too minimal or too overwhelming for other people to handle. Families of people who died by suicide, overdose, homicide, autoerotic asphyxiation, AIDS, or the death penalty experience a double burden: forced to navigate loss while experiencing the guilt or shame that comes from social judgment. When people experience non-death losses related to behaviors that society does not widely accept or endorse, these too receive less attention and support. If the circumstances are not within acceptable standards, most individuals will hesitate to seek support, fearing judgment or rejection.

DISENFRANCHISED GRIEF REACTIONS

Unfortunately, societal expectations do not accommodate the diverse ways people deal with loss. If you grieve without tears, you are "too detached." If you are more expressive, you are "too dramatic." My thanatology professor, Dr Terry Martin, and his colleague, Dr Ken Doka, describe a spectrum of grieving styles. On one end are instrumental grievers, who channel their feelings into physical activities, problem-solving, or projects, seeking practical ways to manage their grief. This may include learning about grief theory, building a memorial, or starting a cause-based movement. On the other end of the spectrum, intuitive grievers express grief through emotion. They tell the story to whoever will listen, they cry on their friends' shoulders. We are the wailers, the people that go through cases and cases of tissues.

In Western society, instrumental grief is viewed as "masculine," while intuitive is seen as "feminine." However, we know that men can cry, and women sometimes don't. Unfortunately, if your style of grieving doesn't match societal gender expectations, you might be unfairly judged as grieving too much or not enough. Cultural norms further complicate this, as what's considered appropriate grieving behavior varies widely across different societies.[3]

SHOWING UP FOR YOURSELF

Disenfranchised grief can also be turned inward. I know firsthand how easy it can be to see your own loss through the lens of dismissive societal views. For a time, I minimized my grief over our marriage ending because it wasn't a death, and after all I am the one who left, even though it was for self-preservation. I still have to defend my grief to myself and others whenever someone asks the innocent yet cringy question, "Were you two close?" when I talk about my uncle or stepfather. Consciously I know I have the right to grieve whatever feels like a loss, and yet social norms are hard to reprogram. But that does not mean we should not try.

When we disenfranchise our own grief, we hinder our ability to adapt, learn, and grow. Learning to honor your loss and trust yourself again is hard, but necessary. I am saying this from both personal and professional experience. Loss robs us of the illusion of control we often believe we have over things we do not. And there are so many things that you can control that you don't yet realize you can. Mastery over your response to the loss—the visceral, emotional reactions it brings about—often lies beyond our grasp.

The rawness of grief, the anger, the disbelief, and the sorrow are not choices; they are instinctive responses to the vacuum left by loss. While you may not be able to control these initial *reactions*, you will, with time and intention, learn to *respond* to them with wisdom and compassion. Recognizing the distinction between reactions and responses—while owning your ability to consciously shape the latter—marks the beginning of a profound journey toward self-trust.

RETURNING HOME TO HERSELF

After she broke up with Richard, Dominique tried to escape her feelings through online dating. It didn't work. She hit rock bottom, emotionally, and knew she had to face her pain to move forward in her life. She dove into yoga, mindfulness meditation, and breathwork using tools she learned from me in Awaken, as well as biofield tuning—a sound therapy that calms the nervous system—to return home to herself.

Dominique told me, "Through this non-death, traumatic experience came a huge learning of self-dignity, self-respect, and self-love. I committed to doing things for myself that I had wanted to do for years but never ended up doing because my life revolved around him. I went on my first ever yoga retreat, which was life-changing! I committed to a regular yoga and self-care schedule. A part of self-love is honoring your own boundaries. Boundaries are there for a reason. However, without this experience, I would have never learned to truly love all aspects of who I am. I am enough, I am worthy, and I do deserve the best ... all statements that I didn't believe until after I experienced this loss of 'the love of my life.'"

To learn to respond wisely to what is beyond our control, we must cultivate an awareness of our internal experiences and recognize our capacity to choose our next steps. This means we can acknowledge our emotions without letting them dictate our actions. There is freedom to be found in the act of choice—how we want to move forward, how we wish to honor our loss, and how we aim to rebuild a sense of trust in ourselves and the world around us. By learning to pause and choose, we reclaim our agency. It's in learning to navigate this space—between stimulus and response—that our power lies.

Just as the hiker at the beginning of this chapter struggled with the weight on their back, unseen by those passing by, so too do those navigating the path of disenfranchised grief carry burdens that are often invisible to others. In the face of misunderstanding and isolation, Dominique's decision to lean into supports like yoga, meditation, and the compassionate community of her grief support group represents the crucial act of setting down her backpack, if only for a moment, to tend to her needs. Her story underscores the importance of acknowledging our grief, regardless of its visibility, and seeking out those who understand the significance of our losses.

Like Dominique, when you are able to honor your loss and tend to your pain, you will feel the load lighten. It may not change the story, nor will it put things back the way they were. But it will help you feel less overwhelmed, and more empowered. Just start by telling yourself, "My loss matters."

REFLECTING ON YOUR DISENFRANCHISED GRIEF

Investigating your experience of loss in relationship to yourself and your support systems is your best first step in navigating grief. Your journal is a safe space to acknowledge the importance of any losses that are disenfranchised by others or yourself.

The prompts below will help you investigate each of the five types of disenfranchised grief. If you do not feel a particular prompt applies to you, skip it and move to the next one that does. As you write, allow your authentic feelings to flow, knowing that there is no right or wrong way to express them. Forget about grammar, spelling, or the need to sound a certain way.

HAVE YOU EXPERIENCED A DISENFRANCHISED LOSS?

- Describe a loss that feels meaningful to you but is disenfranchised by others.

- How does this loss affect your daily life, challenge your assumptions about the world, and influence your feelings about the future? What do you wish others understood about its significance?

EXPLORE THIS: Express why this loss matters to you by writing a story, drawing a picture, or making a collage. Seek out social connections or groups that recognize and support these types of losses.

DO YOU FEEL LIKE A DISENFRANCHISED GRIEVER?

- Describe how your age, abilities, or societal expectations have impacted the support you receive and your ability to ask for help.

- What do you wish people knew about your capacity to experience grief and the importance of receiving supportive, understanding care?

EXPLORE THIS: Advocate for your needs by expressing how meaningful and healing supportive gestures can be. Educate those around you about the complexities of grief, emphasizing that it transcends age, ability, and societal expectations.

WERE YOU INVOLVED IN A DISENFRANCHISED RELATIONSHIP?

- Describe a relationship that has ended or changed, which you feel has been minimized by your support system.

- What do you wish people understood about the depth and significance of this relationship to you, especially regarding its impact on your sense of identity and emotional well-being?

EXPLORE THIS: Honor the connection by creating a memory box or a journal dedicated to capturing stories and moments from this relationship. Sharing your feelings with someone who understands or finding a supportive community can provide comfort and validation.

HAVE YOU EXPERIENCED DISENFRANCHISED CIRCUMSTANCES?

- Describe how the circumstances of your loss are perceived by others and how their responses have affected your grieving process.

- What do you wish people understood about the complexity of your loss beyond the surface-level details, especially the profound emotional and psychological impact it has had on you?

EXPLORE THIS: Connect with people who have experienced a very similar loss. Finding a community or support group that understands the unique nature of your grief can offer a sense of solidarity and understanding.

HAVE YOU HAD A DISENFRANCHISED GRIEF REACTION?

- Describe how your way of grieving has been perceived as being too much or too little.

- What do you wish others knew about the validity and authenticity of your grief response, regardless of how it compares to societal expectations or norms?

EXPLORE THIS: Embrace your unique way of grieving and seek out support that respects your individual style. A therapist or counselor can provide understanding and guidance, helping you navigate your grief in a way that feels right for you.

CHAPTER 2

THE LANGUAGE
OF LOSS

NAMING WHAT SCARES YOU

When we relegate feelings that scare us to a dark corner of our inner world, afraid to speak of them, much less examine them, they grow stronger and more powerful and can feel extra scary.

This concept is illustrated in the Harry Potter series. The supervillain is initially referred to only as "He who shall not be named" because the other characters came to believe that simply naming him could provoke misfortune. Ironically, this refusal to speak of him directly only enhanced his notoriety as a specter of great fear.

Your experience of grief operates in a similar way. Emotions, including pain, are potent messengers signaling that something within demands your attention. Neglect them, and just like "He who shall not be named," they will grow stronger and more powerful. Avoiding your emotions doesn't make them disappear. Instead, they leak out in unexpected ways—an unease you can't quite identify that leaves you feeling unsettled in your own body.

Like Lord Voldemort (there, I said it), that sensation echoing through your being has a name: grief. As soon as you name it, it becomes more manageable because you are no longer grappling with an unknown entity. What if you take this a step further and name the type of grief you are experiencing, along with the specific feelings of sadness, anger, or fear? Naming your grief is like moving the monster from the shadows into the spotlight, where you may see it isn't so scary after all, but scared, tired, and in need of help. And in revealing the source of your fear, you can diminish its power over you.

GRIEF LITERACY

Grief literacy describes the practice of teaching people the essential concepts and skills needed to navigate their own grief and offer meaningful support to others who are adapting to loss. This movement emphasizes understanding how grief can manifest across various dimensions of our lives—physically, mentally, emotionally, behaviorally, and within our relationships and communities. It encourages us all to learn how to show up for ourselves and others in a way that is authentic, compassionate, and free of judgment. As the word "literacy" implies, the "language" of grief is something we can learn. Grief literacy begins with normalizing the experience of loss.

The documentary *Speaking Grief* explores what it is like to lose a relative in a death- and grief- avoidant society. According to Lindsey Whissel Fenton, the documentary's producer and director, "Navigating a loss without grief literacy leaves us vulnerable to problematic misconceptions. We can end up internalizing harmful messaging and using it as a guide for our experience, which often results in us believing that we're doing our grief 'wrong.' This adds the unnecessary weight of guilt, shame, and frustration to an already heavy experience."

Although *Speaking Grief* focuses on death-related loss, Fenton believes that recognizing the grief involved in non-death loss is the foundation of creating a more grief-aware society. She adds that a lack of grief literacy isn't just harmful to grieving people—it can also be detrimental to their support networks. "Despite the experience of grief being a natural, normal part of being human, it is deeply misunderstood. And that misunderstanding hurts us all. It hurts us when we grieve, and it hurts us when we try to support people we care about as they grieve. I've found that when a disconnect happens after any type of loss, it's usually because of a lack of knowing rather than a lack of caring." Fenton reminds us that grief literacy is something we can develop: "No one taught us how to navigate this space, so it makes sense that we don't know what to do. But, as with any skill, grief literacy can be learned."[4]

TYPES OF GRIEF AND LOSS

Grief is an umbrella term of sorts. Beneath it are specific types of grief—how the loss manifests in your being, and different kinds of losses—the source of your grief. Below are more terms to help you grow your grief vocabulary. As you read through the definitions, understand that any one loss may fall into different, even seemingly paradoxical categories. And please know that naming your grief is not labeling your experience as pathological or unhealthy. Quite the opposite. Naming your grief lets you acknowledge the validity of your feelings and honor that in its many forms, grief is a natural part of the human experience. Like all tools, naming your grief is not a should, it is an option if you find it helpful.

What truly matters is not the label itself, but how you use this knowledge to find the most suitable tools and support for your specific type of loss. Whether through support groups, engaging in therapeutic activities, or learning from books and podcasts, finding resources that resonate with your personal experience is crucial.

In the previous chapter you learned about one of the most common forms of grief associated with non-death and non-traditional death-centered losses—disenfranchised grief (see page 25). On the following pages are more definitions, along with examples, so you can clearly identify and speak about your grief.

ANTICIPATORY GRIEF

Anticipatory grief describes the experience of loss that happens prior to a death or major life change. This is most often associated with expected life-limiting illnesses, but can also apply to non-death losses such as divorce, migration, and even perceived joyous events such as retirement. Therese A. Rando, in her 1986 publication "Anticipatory Grief: The Term Is a Misnomer but the Phenomenon Exists," highlighted this type of grief, bringing attention to how individuals might grapple with the loss of everyday experiences and independence, such as a loved one's ability to drive or perform personal care tasks, before the person dies.[5] It's a complex mix of emotions, including sadness, anxiety, and fear about the future without the person or thing we're about to lose.

SUFFOCATED GRIEF

Suffocated grief occurs when an individual's grief is not only disenfranchised—lacking acknowledgment or support—but also penalized or criticized. Coined by Dr Tashel Bordere, a certified thanatologist and assistant professor at the University of Missouri-Columbia, suffocated grief is commonly experienced by marginalized people, for example a person of color, victim of a violent crime, or member of the LGBTQ+ community. This can occur in various systems, such as healthcare, workplaces, schools, and prisons, and through interactions with individuals or groups.

Consider Jamal, a 12-year-old African-American boy, who experienced the traumatic loss of his home due to a fire. In the aftermath, he becomes alternately angry, restless, and sleepy in class, and has trouble focusing on his schoolwork. Instead of recognizing these behaviors as normal grief reactions, his school misinterprets them as disciplinary issues and places him in a special education class. Unfortunately, this happens quite often to children with less privileged backgrounds, and can extend to adults as well.

"I want to acknowledge that all bereaved populations deal with some level of disenfranchisement." Dr Bordere shared in an interview with Fenton. "We all know what it's like to experience a loss and go back to our workplaces or go back to the gym or wherever we operate and have people not acknowledge our losses… It's one thing to not have your loss acknowledged. It's another to be penalized for your grief expression. That's further isolating."[6]

TANGIBLE AND INTANGIBLE LOSS

Tangible and intangible losses are differentiated by their ability to be quantified or easily perceived. Tangible losses are those that are more obvious, often concrete and measurable, and include changes in physical health, work status, resources, and housing, among others. Conversely, intangible, unseen, or invisible losses are often more symbolic or more abstract, including loss of social status, sense of control, security, safety, innocence, dignity, faith, dreams, or changes in identity. Although these losses are often invisible to others, they deeply impact an individual's sense of self and assumptive worldview.

There is often an overlap between these two types of loss, illustrating how intertwined our emotional and material worlds can be. When our marriage ended due to my husband's chronic financial infidelity—a term I didn't know prior but know all too well now—our divorce meant we had to sell our home and use a good bit of the proceeds to pay off debts (tangible losses). And the humiliation of the betrayal cut deep, leaving me feeling embarrassed, vulnerable, unloved, and sad over losing the shared future I once envisioned (intangible losses). The financial instability shook the very foundations of the life I thought we were building together. Our history, stretching back to our teenage years and full of countless shared memories, now felt like a collection of moments turned to ash.

Being a grief professional does not exempt me from the very human pain of loss. What it does do is surround me with a grief-literate friend group that I could lean into. I also used the tools I am teaching you in this book. Today, I am so much happier and more secure than I have ever been because I went through this. But that does not mean I am immune to the pangs of grief that may resurface from time to time. It simply means I've equipped myself with the knowledge and strategies to navigate these moments and trust that I will make it through.

AMBIGUOUS LOSS

Ambiguous loss, a concept developed by Pauline Boss, Professor Emeritus at the University of Minnesota, describes the profound uncertainty felt when a loved one's presence or absence isn't clear. This type of loss occurs in scenarios when individuals, such as those who have run away from home, have been abducted, are missing in action, or are birth mothers within the adoption triad, remain physically absent yet emotionally and psychologically present. Conversely, individuals who are physically present but psychologically absent, such as those battling dementia or addiction, represent the inverse of this loss. Their physical presence contrasts sharply with the psychological absence of their former selves, overshadowed by illness or substance dependence.

The process of coming out and transitioning can lead to a type of ambiguous loss for both transgender individuals and their families. Even though the person is physically present, the psychological changes they undergo can create a sense of loss. This feeling may be experienced by the transgender person as they navigate their new identity, and by their family and friends as they adjust to the changes. The intensity of this loss often varies depending on the level of support from their social circles.

These situations challenge traditional notions of grief, as there is often no closure or clear resolution. The ambiguity makes it difficult for those affected to move forward, as they find themselves caught between hope and the reality of their situation.[7]

LIVING LOSS

When a person dies, the event of their death is a singular, finite occurrence. Following this, loved ones go through a deep period of mourning with grief that can surface unexpectedly throughout their lives. However, over time, most people find ways to adjust, aided by support systems and natural coping mechanisms that help diminish grief's intensity. Living losses are ongoing and deeply felt, requiring continual adaptation. They often arise when we come to realize that our life has not unfolded as we had hoped, and our plans, dreams, and aspirations have not been realized.

For instance, many of my friends, now in midlife, are facing the lost dream of having their own biological children. I met a woman recently who shared her sorrow over her aging legs, which now prevent her from walking on her beloved beach—a place she visits yearly with her family and that holds precious memories. These are all living losses, reflecting the ongoing adjustments we are asked to make as our circumstances change.[8]

NONFINITE LOSS

Nonfinite losses are a particular type of living loss. They are often precipitated by a significant life event that has lasting physical or psychological effects. A surgeon who loses the use of her hands, or a person diagnosed with a chronic neurological disease. Another example is divorce, where the legal dissolution of the marriage might be finalized quickly, but the two parties must meet regularly to coparent. Nonfinite losses continually affect the individual's life, with daily reminders, and require constant adaptation to persistent reminders of the loss. There is often ongoing uncertainty, anxiety, and a sense of helplessness or powerlessness that can lead to feelings of shame and embarrassment.[9]

PRACTICE:
CHARTING YOUR GRIEF TIMELINE

Your grief timeline is a visible record of the losses you have experienced throughout your lifespan. Even though you may be well aware of the grief you are now facing, it is possible that previous losses may be minimized or overlooked. Creating a timeline not only helps you assess what has been lost, but how facing these difficulties has impacted your assumptive world and patterns.

This exercise is not just about documenting losses; it's about honoring the complex tapestry of your life's experiences. It's a testament to your resilience, a recognition of your grief, and an acknowledgment of the continuous journey of healing and growth. Let this timeline be a reminder of your strength, the depth of your experiences, and your capacity for renewal amid the ebb and flow of life.

MATERIALS NEEDED

- A large piece of paper or a journal spread
- Colored pencils or markers in various colors
- A ruler (optional, for those who prefer straight lines)

PREPARE YOURSELF

1. Settle into a quiet, comfortable space where you won't be disturbed. Take a few deep breaths to center yourself, acknowledging the courage it takes to embark on this journey of reflection. Consider the many types of death and non-death losses you have experienced in your life, including:

- Relationships
- Health
- Financial Security
- Physical Safety
- Emotional Safety
- Identity
- Dreams/Expectations
- Home/Sense of Place
- Purpose/Meaning
- Career/Hobbies

CREATE YOUR TIMELINE

2. Orient your paper horizontally, and draw a straight line across the center, dividing the top and bottom in half. This line represents your lifeline from birth until the present moment.

3. Divide your line into four equal parts, marking each point with your pen or pencil. Label the leftmost point with your birthdate, and the rightmost point with the current year. Make another mark in the middle of the line and label that as the year between your birth and the age you are now.

RECORD YOUR LOSSES

4. Create a color-coded key using different colors to represent various types of losses. For example, blue for relationship losses (divorce, breakup), green for health-related losses (illness, disability), yellow for tangible losses (career, financial losses), and so on.

5. Record your losses by placing a colored mark along the timeline, and label each event with the date and name of what you lost.

COLOR YOUR RESILIENCE

6. Choose a color that represents resilience, growth, or healing for you. Start with a mark indicating when you purchased this book, as it is a sign of hope. Record these positive, expansive moments by placing a mark in your chosen color along the timeline, and label each event with the date and name of what you gained.

REFLECT ON PATTERNS AND INSIGHTS

7. Once you've mapped out your losses, take a step back. Observe any patterns or clusters of losses. Reflect on the following questions, journaling your responses:

- What emotions surfaced as you completed your timeline?

- Are there periods in your life with concentrated losses, and if so, how did you cope during those times?

- How have different types of losses impacted you in various stages of your life?

- Can you identify any periods of growth or significant change that followed these losses?

CHAPTER 3

MINDFUL TOOLS FOR YOUR HEALING JOURNEY

THE OPPORTUNITY IN A CRISIS

Navigating loss is a lot less scary when you have a toolkit of coping skills and self-care practices to help you cope with stress and build resilience. Just knowing you have something to do when big feelings arise can make you feel more in control of your experience. Coping skills are on-the-spot behaviors that reduce your distress.

As a pre-teen, I was told that I didn't have any healthy coping skills. I internalized this condemnation and, from that point on, carried a belief that I was destined to suffer. Little Me did not understand that such skills are *learned* behaviors. She certainly didn't know there was a difference between healthy and unhealthy coping, much less what healthy coping skills might look like. So, she/I spent many years drawing upon the "skills" I was familiar with—using avoidance, alcohol, food, and dysfunctional relationships to numb my pain.

On the surface, I was the picture of success. At 26, I started a web development company that employed ten people and had a boyfriend and a solid social life. But underneath there was a chronic distress that eventually manifested in my body as shingles. When my nurse practitioner gave me the news, she handed me a prescription and made what was a radical suggestion in the year 2001: try yoga.

That September, I attended my first yoga retreat at the Kripalu Center in Massachusetts. Fifteen days before the retreat was scheduled to start, the country was rocked by the 9/11 attacks. My partner at the time begged me not to go, afraid that something bad would happen to me, but I knew I had to do this for my body and my heart.

Many of my fellow retreatants had lost family, friends, or coworkers in the Twin Towers, and the facilitator did an amazing job of holding space for everyone's story while giving us things to do with our pain other than ruminate. We moved. We journaled. We cried, and laughed. Two decades later, and I remember the waves of grief that released through my body while I stood with my arms raised in tadasana, yoga's mountain pose, quivering and sobbing but grounded.

I cried over my Uncle Doug, who died by suicide when I was seven, for my struggle with bulimia and denial of my own body's screams. I grieved for my parents' divorce. I also wept for the global suffering of 9/11 and for my classmates' grief about their lost loved ones. It was an ugly cry, which for me, is the sweetest kind. When I could no longer stand, I dropped to the ground in child's pose, then rolled onto my side, and rested.

This somatic release—the letting go of tension and trauma stored within my tissues—brought me back home to my body's wisdom. I realized in that moment that I had ignored my body, but my body had not ignored me. Everything I experienced was imprinted inside of me. My body knew things my consciousness did not. That weekend, I rekindled my relationship with myself. I understood that my body and mind were in constant communication. I accepted that though there are many changes in life beyond my control, I have more power to nurture myself than I had ever realized.

What began as a health crisis was the springboard I needed to learn healthy coping skills and self-care practices (because as an adult, I now understand what was not known to Little Me—healthy coping skills are learnable). Some of my favorites are counting from ten down to one before I respond to a difficult email, walking outside when I feel overwhelmed, and giving myself a ten-minute break to cry when I feel sadness bubbling up in my stomach but I need to do work.

This health crisis also led me to a new career. In the year that followed, I sold my web development company to a dear friend and started training to be a Phoenix Rising Yoga Therapist (PRYT), a modality grounded in yoga, Buddhism, psychology, and neuroscience. The guiding principle of PRYT is that you already have what you need inside of you, and that a compassionate practitioner can help you cultivate a state of self-awareness that leads to wisdom *and* action.

YOUR TOOLKIT FOR NAVIGATING LOSS

Self-care practices are regularly scheduled activities that help mitigate day-to-day stress by allowing you to recharge and nurture your well-being. My current self-care routine includes morning meditation followed by journaling at least 750 words, starting with the prompt: how am I really doing today, and what do I need? I also hike on the Chesapeake & Ohio Canal Towpath—a dirt trail that runs alongside the Potomac River—with my dog at least four days a week, go to personal training at the gym twice a week, and get a massage once a month.

Your self-care may look completely different based on your time, resources, and needs—as it should. Self-care should include things that feel nourishing to you, not what someone else tells you to do. How often should you practice? The research suggests that it is better to do a little something every day then binge-practice once a week. So, if you are not already scheduling time for self-care, start small. Even five minutes of mindful movement, meditation, or journaling will help you reconnect with yourself and tend to your core needs. In addition to that, carve out one to two hours a week to go a little deeper with any of the exercises you choose. It is more important that you lean into the practices you find most useful than the ones you feel you "should" do; the last thing self-care should do is increase your stress by adding yet another activity that feels obligatory to your to-do list. There is no one right way to learn how to live with loss, but there are many possibilities.

The emphasis here is on the word practice. Perfection is not the goal and striving for it can be frustrating and exhausting and defeats the purpose. Just as you don't need to cook a gourmet meal to satisfy your hunger, you don't need to master these practices to experience their benefits. And be sure to give yourself the patience you deserve. Our society may value quick-fixes and forward motion, but you are not on anyone else's timeline. The research varies on how long it takes to form a new habit, anywhere from a few weeks to a few months. But even if it is the latter, the time invested is just a drop in the bucket when you consider that you are building skills not just for now, but for a lifetime.

Allow yourself to adapt. The human brain is amazingly flexible. Neuroplasticity is the process through which we can literally rewire our minds; reprogramming yours to cope with distress in a skillful way is a lot like breaking in new hiking boots. At first, it is hard to give up your old, reliable boots, no matter how worn-out they are. But even though the new pair are stiff and uncomfortable at first, the more you use them, the better they feel. Your unconscious mind will resist replacing old habits with new, even when your habits are harmful or unhelpful. But all it takes is repetition, time, and positive emotion to free yourself from the grip of old patterns and embrace new, healthier ways of coping. Just as those new hiking boots eventually conform to your feet, healthy coping will become your second nature.

BALANCING GRIEF AND RESTORATION

Remember our metaphorical hiker from Chapter 1? Let's replace them with an actual hiker: me. The first and only time I went backcountry hiking with the intention of camping was in 1996 in the Shenandoah Forest. My best friend and my boyfriend claimed to be experienced campers. I was a complete newbie and they reluctantly allowed me to invite myself along.

Our plan was to hike an 11-mile loop and stop halfway to camp for the night. While my friend registered us with the ranger station, I read the wall plaque that detailed what to do if you encountered a bear. We were only a mile in when I learned that "*when* you encounter a bear" is more apt than "*if* you encounter a bear."

We dutifully employed the tips from the plaque, clapping and yelling "Hey bear!" at the cutest mama and her cubs we stumbled upon during the opening stretch of our trek. Even though our tactic worked and the bears scampered off, my friend had a panic attack, citing her fear that we might see more bears. My boyfriend also began exhibiting signs of anxiety. Considering I was the newbie, I remained surprisingly calm. I tried to comfort them by reminding them that we had bear-repelling skills, but nothing seemed to help. A unilateral decision was made to hike back to the car, even though it meant climbing the rocky terrain in the dark of night.

This required both physical skill and mental focus and frequent periods of rest. There was one time when my friend sat on rocks and cried, saying we should just leave her and keep going, but we didn't. There were times when my legs hurt so bad I didn't think I could keep going, but I did. There were times when we imagined seeing bears in the dark, and we sang what seemed like 10,000 rounds of "100 Bottles of Beer on the Wall" to scare them off and help us keep our mind off our fears. Four hours later we made it back to the car. I fell to my knees and kissed the pavement.

During that hike, I had to balance focusing on navigating the difficult path and taking frequent breaks to rest my body. I had to scan for bears and distract my mind with a silly song so I wasn't afraid. Basically, I continuously moved between doing the work (hiking and scanning) and taking a break (resting and singing).

Navigating grief requires a similar approach. Confronting the reality of your loss and avoiding it so you can rebuild your life is at the heart of what's known as the Dual Process Model of Coping with Bereavement. This explains that loss-orientated tasks include doing your grief work, tending to the intrusion of grief, relinquishing/continuing/relocating your bond with the person who died, and denying or avoiding the myriad of changes. Restoration-oriented tasks include attending to those changes, doing new things, distracting yourself from grief, and adapting to new roles, identities, and relationships.[10]

Originally developed to explain the experience of death-related grief, this model was adapted to non-death loss by Dr Darcy Harris. She modified loss-orientated tasks to include shattered assumptions, reminders of the loss, chronic sorrow, disequilibrium, and awareness of impermanence, and altered restoration-oriented tasks to encompass new perspectives, attending to daily life, accommodation/rebuilding, and awareness of possibilities.

Observing your movement between loss-oriented and restoration-oriented tasks will give you a holistic view of your grief journey. It helps you see that oscillating between these two polarities will give you insight into your complex emotional landscape. This ebb and flow is not about right or wrong; it's about understanding the diverse ways you are learning to live with your loss. Allow yourself this awareness without judgment, seeing it as a comprehensive reflection of your healing process.

PRACTICE:
BUILDING HEALTHY COPING SKILLS

An emotion is made up of three parts:

- a subjective experience that activates a memory or belief;

- a physiological response that shows up as a feeling in the body;

- a behavioral response that is designed to help you adapt to and survive the situation.

This will help you understand that between the physiological response and the behavioral response is an opportunity to pause and choose a healthy coping skill over an unhealthy one.

CHOOSING HEALTHY COPING SKILLS

The following list offers suggestions for alternative actions you can choose to make in your behavior if you can bring awareness to your responses.

- Take a deep breath instead of lashing out at someone.

- Count from ten down to one instead of reacting impulsively.

- Notice your feet on the floor instead of spiraling into panic.

- Name five objects in the room you are in instead of getting lost in overwhelming thoughts.

- Visualize a safe place or person instead of dwelling on negative scenarios.

- Take a walk instead of sitting with escalating stress.

- Look at a funny picture or video instead of ruminating on problems.

- Pet your companion animal instead of feeling isolated.

- Stretch your arms over your head instead of holding on to physical tension.

- Write how you feel in your journal instead of suppressing your emotions.

- Do puzzles instead of overthinking stress-inducing issues.

- Read instead of endlessly scrolling through social media.

- Call a friend instead of bottling up your feelings.

- Play an upbeat song instead of succumbing to a mood slump.

- Imagine you are wrapped in a protective light instead of feeling vulnerable and exposed.

- Place your hand over your heart instead of criticizing yourself.

- Massage your shoulders or arms instead of enduring stress-induced discomfort.

- Suck on a mint instead of smoking or other nervous habits.

- Drink mint or cinnamon tea instead of consuming caffeine or alcohol when stressed.

- Offer yourself comforting words instead of engaging in negative self-talk.

Use your journal to reflect on one moment every day for 21 days to track your emotional reactions and the choices you make in response. This practice can help you become more aware of your patterns and the effectiveness of different coping strategies in real-life situations.

REVIEW THE SITUATION AND YOUR RESPONSE

1. Your subjective experience: What event or thought initiated the stress?

2. Your physiological response: What did you notice happening in your body and mind?

3. Your behavioral response: What action did you take to manage the feelings, whether skillful or not?

REFLECT IN YOUR JOURNAL

4. If your reaction was less than ideal, treat yourself with kindness. Think about how you might respond differently in similar situations ahead. Write in your journal: *The next time I feel [emotion], instead of [unskillful reaction], I can choose to [skillful reaction].*

5. If you navigated the situation well, celebrate this success. Reflect on how this skillful approach felt different compared to past times when you might not have responded as well, both in your body and mind. Write in your journal: *When I responded skillfully by [describe your action], I noticed [describe the physical and mental sensation]. This experience teaches me [insight or lesson learned].*

REVIEW YOUR PROGRESS

6. At the end of 21 days, reflect on the changes in your stress management and any shifts in your emotional well-being. Remember, the goal is progress, not perfection. By observing, reflecting, and intentionally choosing your responses, you're learning to dance gracefully with stress.

With this exercise, you're not just reacting to stress; you're actively engaging with it in a way that cultivates strength and resilience. Keep in mind that every step is a lesson, and with each lesson, you're adding more graceful steps to your stress dance. Welcome each day as an opportunity to refine your movements and remember, you are the choreographer of your own calm.

CHAPTER 4

TENDING TO YOUR GRIEVING BODY

WHY WE ARE AFRAID TO FEEL

Have you ever been afraid to feel? I know I have. Because emotions are felt in your body, this fear of turning inward can prevent you from understanding what your body truly needs.

When I moved into my riverside home prior to my divorce, I spent my days unpacking, organizing, working, and generally feeling productive and liberated. However, when I took time to pay attention to how I really felt during my daily meditation practice or while walking along the Potomac River feelings of sadness, fear, and anxiety would start to rise to the surface. At times I was afraid that if I let myself really experience these emotions I would fall into a deep well of sorrow from which I might not emerge. I also felt ashamed of the idea that anyone might think I was weak, or that I couldn't cope.

Even though I knew I had the tools to tend to my suffering, like you, I am a human being, and grief hurts. So in those early months I found skillful (and sometimes not so skillful) ways to distract myself from my pain, because I was too tender and not yet grounded enough to sit with my feelings. One afternoon, while swimming in the Potomac in front of my new home, I stood up in the shallow part of the river and reached my arms overhead into mountain pose. Grief poured out of my body, just like it did at the Kripalu Retreat in 2001. This time it was over the loss of my marriage, and for the healthy relationship I crave, but will never have, with my father. And just like before, there was a sense of relief that I could be honest with myself about how I really felt.

It is hard to pinpoint why I felt safe enough to meet my grief at that moment; all I can say is that I was ready. Maybe it was because my body remembered that I had been able to turn toward what hurt before, and still emerge unscathed. Maybe it was the serene setting, the gentle flow of the river around me, providing a sense of connection to nature and the present moment that allowed me to let go. Whatever the reason, the emotion I released was not a conscious choice, but a natural kind of awakening. I allowed myself to feel the full weight of my grief without judgment or fear. It was a transformative moment of embracing my vulnerability and courage—and a sense of strength found in surrender.

THE PHYSICAL TOLL OF GRIEF

Since grief can feel like a threat to your survival, it activates your body's stress response, also known as fight-flight-freeze-fawn. This is an unconscious reaction programmed into your body to help keep you safe when you sense danger. You are likely familiar with fight-or-flight—the instinct to either confront or flee from a threat. Somewhat less known are freeze and fawn. Like an animal that plays dead to evade a predator, freeze renders you unable to move. Fawn is the act of trying to please or appease the threat; it's a trauma response and is not uncommon in abusive relationships. All of these stress responses release a cascade of hormones, including adrenaline and glucocorticoids, and activate systems in your body to enhance alertness, while simultaneously deactivating those that are unnecessary when facing a threat.

For example, your heart rate speeds up to send more blood to your muscles, preparing you for action. At the same time, your digestion slows because your body doesn't prioritize processing food when survival is at stake. This survival mechanism is wired into the nervous systems of all vertebrates, including mammals like dogs and cats, as well as birds, fish, and reptiles. But there is a key difference between critters and people that impacts how we each respond to stress: the complexity of the human brain.

Humans are prone to rumination. Our minds try to understand why something happened, what we should do in response, and how to prevent similar things from happening in the future. In addition to a general sense of being on edge, this relentless mental churning can lead to appetite changes, sleep disturbances, inflammation, and/or other physical symptoms like headaches, joint pain, and stomach issues, among others. These manifestations of grief that show up in your body are called somatization: the expression of psychological distress through physical symptoms. What may surprise you is that not all creatures experience this.

Many animals have more primal methods of releasing stress from their bodies. They don't ruminate and worry like we do. Instead, they do things like shake or run or perform some other physical movement that serves like a pressure valve for that nervous energy. This prevents trauma from embedding in their nervous system and allows them to recover without lingering effects. They react to stressful stimuli in the moment, release, and move on, meaning they are spared from the wear and tear on their physical and emotional body that we humans experience.

Trauma therapist Peter Levine noted this phenomenon and pondered if and how this clever adaptation in animals could also be utilized by humans. His observation and study ultimately led Levine to develop what is now known as Somatic Experiencing (SE). This is a therapeutic approach that encourages us to reconnect with our body's innate ability to release trauma by focusing on bodily sensations and engaging in physical activities that discharge stress.

While you might choose to seek out an SE practitioner, a trauma therapist, or a Phoenix Rising Yoga Therapist like me to address the physical manifestations of trauma, there are also many things you can do on your own to release the residual stress lodged in your body. Cardiovascular exercise will increase your heart rate and help you dispel some of that traumatic energy. Twenty minutes a day of an activity like dancing, speed walking, running, or yoga, can significantly reduce stress levels—yes, you can literally shake it off. (Always consult with your healthcare practitioner before starting any new exercise regimen.)

This type of movement along with eating nutritious food, drinking water, and good sleep hygiene, are what I call the Four Givens. Together, they form the foundation that every human needs to have a healthy life. Additionally, relaxation techniques such as spending time in nature, deep breathing, progressive muscle relaxation, peaceful visualization, or immersing yourself in a creative activity can help reverse the harmful effects of stress. The Four Givens become even more important when you are constantly barraged with stress, such as when you're grieving.

WINDOW OF TOLERANCE

There is nothing wrong—and everything right—with approaching your pain gradually and in your own time. Words like denial, avoidance, and acceptance are tossed around all too often by those who have never felt the deep pain of loss, in my opinion. And while it is not healthy to suppress pain indefinitely, we all have a limit to how much stress we can handle. When feeling becomes too much, you may fall outside what trauma therapist Dr Dan Siegel refers to as the window of tolerance. This is the optimal zone for emotional regulation. Within this window, you can tend to emotions without becoming overwhelmed (hyperarousal) or dissociated (hypoarousal). Hyperarousal puts you in a state of high alert, where anxiety, panic, and restlessness prevail. Hypoarousal feels numb and detached, and disconnects you from the present. You may feel empty, or like you are floating outside your body.

While not all loss results in a diagnosis of post-traumatic stress disorder, or Trauma with a capital "T," any experience of loss can still feel deeply traumatic. If you find yourself experiencing flashbacks, hallucinations, or losing periods of time due to dissociation, your body is attempting to protect you from a perceived threat, often rooted in past events. In such cases, it is important to seek out a trauma therapist to help you integrate your past experiences in a safe and healthy way. Research suggests that addressing the root cause of trauma should precede or occur alongside grief therapy, ensuring that both emotional and psychological healing are effectively managed.

Learning to recognize when we are outside our window of tolerance is beneficial for everyone. It's important to understand our physical and emotional limits and to be attentive to the physiological cues that signal when we are moving beyond what feels safe. Peter Levine shares a useful approach using the Greek myth of Medusa. You may recall that the snake-headed goddess, a once-beautiful figure turned monstrous, could petrify anyone who looked directly into her eyes. When charged with the seemingly impossible task of defeating her, Perseus chose an indirect method. He used a reflective shield, provided by the goddess Athena, to view her as if in a mirror, thus avoiding the direct gaze that would have turned him to stone. Levine explains that by facing our traumas indirectly, we can observe and process our emotions safely, without becoming paralyzed by them.

EMOTION REGULATION

Emotion regulation can be challenging when you're trying to balance your grief experience with the demands of daily life, such as the care of a relative. The number of adult children (predominantly women) taking on the role of family caregiver for an aging parent is increasing; with that comes novel social, occupational, financial, cognitive, and physical stressors. These can take a significant toll on health and well-being which is often compounded by the heart-wrenching experience of watching a loved one decline and anticipating their death (anticipatory grief, see page 34). Despite these stressors, many informal family caregivers feel like they must stay strong even while falling apart.[11]

STELLA'S STORY:
REGAINING A SENSE OF WELL-BEING

Stella and her mother had what she described as more than a mother/daughter relationship; they were best friends, inseparable in spirit, and attuned to each other no matter how geographically far apart they were. "I suspected she had cancer long before we got the official diagnosis from the doctor. I just kept it to myself and buried my anxiety and fear around my suspicions deep within myself. But when the doctor confirmed my suspicions, I knew I had a long and difficult road ahead of me."

Given their strong bond, it was an easy decision for Stella to become her mother's primary caregiver. But this decision required Stella to quit her job in order to stay in her mom's home and marked the beginning of an emotionally and physically demanding journey.

"She worsened pretty quickly and had an enormous amount of physical pain. She was always at risk for falling and couldn't bathe without help. I knew it was only a matter of time. In the beginning I was so busy caring for her that I tried to just stay strong and efficient in her presence, but I would cry in private."

As her mother's condition deteriorated, so did Stella's well-being. "I cried a lot, and I felt a deep ache and pain in my chest. It was my heart breaking." Her description of both the physical and metaphorical state of her heart illustrates how the somatization of grief is so prevalent that it is a part of our everyday language. She was profoundly exhausted, but she couldn't sleep. She wasn't hungry. And the anxiety was overwhelming. "I lived in fear and this sense of impending doom. Her death was coming and when I thought about it, it would send me into a panic." Each physical symptom echoed her emotional exhaustion, as caregiver stress wore her body down.

Stella found herself struggling to remain strong for her mother while privately crumbling under the constant state of fear and exhaustion. Then came guilt over the fact that, as much as she didn't want to lose her mother, Stella wanted her mom's suffering to end. This added layer of grief only intensified Stella's physical distress and emotional sorrow. "I was losing my best friend. And I was afraid ... The pain and sadness was enormous."

After her mother died, Stella struggled to redirect the energy spent caring for her mother into relearning how to care for herself. The immense pain she felt prior to her mom's death was transformed into numbness in her heart and body. The intense caregiving was over, but that left a void that drained her energy. As is true with many who take on this role, the transition out of the identity of caregiver was challenging.

Over the last year, Stella has regained a sense of well-being and says that she treasures the precious time she had with her mother, no matter how demanding it was at the time. "One of the things that always brings me comfort is that we had so much time to talk before she passed. Perhaps knowing that the end is near gives time and space to say all the things that one would want to say to your loved one."

Stella joined a grief support group for caregivers, drawing comfort from the shared stories of love and loss. She started prioritizing her physical well-being by exercising regularly and sticking to a daily routine that focused on good sleep hygiene. "If I could recommend anything to anyone who is suffering with grief it would be to focus on getting a good night's sleep. Sleeping not only soundly, but all through the night without interruption does wonders for my heart and mind. I find that when I sleep well I have less bouts of deep pain or depression. It doesn't mean that I am not grieving still, I'm just able to meet the demands of my day with more presence and optimism."

PRACTICE:
SOMATIC YOGA THERAPY

This sequence of yoga postures is designed to gently deepen your connection with your body, helping you to release somatic tension associated with grief. You have the choice to approach this series in a way that feels most helpful to you—whether that means engaging with all of the postures as a complete practice, or choosing individual poses that resonate with your current needs. (Always check with your healthcare provider before engaging in any new exercises.)

- Move slowly and with curiosity, allowing yourself to truly experience each sensation. Pause at any time to explore and get curious about the sensations in your body. This mindful approach encourages a deeper engagement with each posture, enhancing the therapeutic benefits of your practice.

- Pay attention to your breath. If you notice that you hold your breath or it becomes rapid, you may be moving beyond your emotional or physical comfort zone, and may need to rest or reset.

- Each posture includes a suggested intention that you can keep in mind while doing it.

- It is more effective to do a little bit of movement each day, rather than one big session each week. Even dedicating just five minutes to moving your body can make a significant difference in feeling more grounded and present.

DIAPHRAGMATIC BREATHING

Breath can calm the nervous system and bring awareness to the present moment, setting a foundation for your practice. If controlling your breath in this way does not feel calming, you can simply breathe in a natural way.

INTENTION: Focus on the sensation of expansion in your breath and body to foster a deep connection with the present moment, allowing grief to flow through you without resistance.

1. Sit or lie down comfortably.

2 Place one hand on your chest and the other on your belly.

3 Slowly breathe in through your nose, feeling your belly rise (not your chest).

4. Exhale slowly through your mouth, feeling your belly fall.

5. Repeat for a few minutes, focusing on deep belly movements.

PELVIC TILTS

Begin to engage the core and lower back gently, warming up the spine and further increasing body awareness.

INTENTION: Cultivate a sense of grounding and stability. As you engage your core, visualize drawing strength from the earth.

1. Lie on your back with knees bent and feet flat on the ground.

2. Flatten your lower back against the floor by gently tilting your pelvis up.

3. Hold for a few seconds, then return to the starting position.

4. Repeat 10–15 times, keeping the movement slow and controlled.

CAT-COW STRETCHES

This fluid movement warms up the spine, as well as encouraging flexibility and breath synchronization.

INTENTION: Embrace flexibility and resilience. With each movement, imagine releasing the stiffness and pain of grief, making room for healing and breath.

1. Start on your hands and knees, with wrists under shoulders and knees under hips.

2. Inhale, drop your belly down, and look up (Cow Pose).

3. Exhale, round your back up toward the ceiling, tucking your chin to your chest (Cat Pose).

4. Flow between these two poses smoothly with your breath for a few minutes.

MOUNTAIN TO FORWARD FOLD FLOW

Transition into a standing position, starting to engage the entire body and encourage a deeper release of tension through the forward fold.

INTENTION: Honor your highs and lows. Recognize that just like your body moves between peaks and valleys, so too does the journey through grief.

1. Stand in Mountain Pose (standing tall, feet hip-width apart).

2. Inhale, raise your arms overhead.

3. Exhale, hinge at your hips, and fold forward, bending your knees as needed.

4. Inhale, rise back up to Mountain Pose.

5. Repeat several times, flowing with your breath.

SHOULDER SHRUGS AND ROLLS

Release tension in the shoulders and neck, areas where stress is commonly held, preparing for deeper stretches.

INTENTION: Recognize how easily tension accumulates and, similarly, how easily it can be released, encouraging a cycle of renewal with each roll.

1. Stand comfortably.

2. Lift your shoulders up toward your ears (shrug), then roll them back and down.

3. Repeat the shrug, then roll forward and down.

4. Continue alternating between back and forward rolls for a few minutes.

LEG WINDSHIELD WIPERS

Return to a lying position for this hip and lower back release, decreasing intensity as you start to move toward more relaxing poses.

INTENTION: Visualize wiping away obstructions like dirt on a windshield, letting go of what no longer serves you while clarifying your vision and perspective with each movement.

1. Lie on your back with knees bent up and feet wider than hip-width on the floor.

2. Gently sway your knees from side to side, like windshield wipers.

3. Move within a comfortable range, aiming for a gentle stretch in your hips and lower back.

4. Continue for a few minutes, following a pace that feels good.

SEATED TWISTS

Introduce gentle twists to both sides to detoxify the body and invigorate the spine, continuing the downshift toward more restorative movements.

INTENTION: Focus on wringing out negative thoughts to make room for positivity, integrating experiences and letting go of what no longer serves you.

1. Sit on the floor with legs extended.

2. Bend your right knee, placing your right foot outside your left knee.

3. Twist your torso to the right, placing your left elbow outside your right knee.

4. Hold for a few breaths, then switch sides.

5. Keep the twist gentle and within a comfortable range.

BUTTERFLY POSE

Shift to a seated stretch that opens the hips and encourages a gentle release, preparing the body for final relaxation.

INTENTION: Embrace transformation with each flutter, opening to the wings of possibility and new beginnings.

1. Sit on the floor, bringing the soles of your feet together and knees out to the sides.

2. Hold your feet with your hands and gently flutter your knees up and down like butterfly wings.

3. Then, staying with knees down, lean forward for a deeper stretch, keeping your back straight.

4. Hold for a few breaths, focusing on opening your hips gently.

CHILD'S POSE

Move into this grounding pose, allowing for introspection and a deep sense of physical relief, beginning the process of closing the practice.

INTENTION: Return to a place of simplicity and security. Use this pose to feel grounded and nurtured as you reconnect with your inner calm.

1. Start on your hands and knees.

2. Sit back on your heels, stretching your arms forward on the floor.

3. Rest your forehead on the ground, relax your shoulders and arms.

4. Stay in this pose for a few minutes, breathing deeply.

RESTING POSE (SAVASANA)

Allow your nervous system to calm and your mind to become quiet, promoting a sense of peace and well-being.

INTENTION: Surrender fully to the moment. Allow the earth to support you completely, trusting that you are held as you rest and rejuvenate.

1. Lie flat on your back, letting your legs fall slightly apart and your arms rest by your sides, palms facing upward.

2. Adjust your position so that you are comfortable and your spine is straight.

3. Close your eyes gently, letting go of any effort to control your breath, allowing your body to breathe naturally.

4. Allow every part of your body to become heavy, sinking into the ground beneath you.

5. Stay in this pose for 5–10 minutes, letting your body and mind absorb the benefits of your practice and rejuvenate deeply.

SOMATIC WALKING MEDITATION

Conclude with this mindful walking practice to integrate the session's benefits, gently transitioning from the yoga practice back into the flow of daily life, while maintaining a heightened sense of bodily awareness and calm.

INTENTION: Walk the path of healing in the present. With each step, affirm your desire to move forward, while honoring your past.

1. Find a safe, quiet space to walk back and forth.

2. Focus on the sensation of each foot as it touches the ground, rolling from heel to toe.

3. Walk slowly, aligning your breath with your steps if possible.

4. Continue for a few minutes, staying present with each step and breath.

CHAPTER 5

MINDFULNESS IN FACING DIFFICULT EMOTIONS

WHAT IS HAPPENING NOW

It is natural to turn away from pain. However, this avoidance only offers temporary relief. Mindfulness, the practice of focusing on the present moment with clarity and compassion, can help you navigate emotional overwhelm and tend to what is happening now in a skillful way. With practice and persistence, you will learn how to cultivate equanimity— a calm and steady mind even in the face of powerful emotions.

Let's head back to the hiking trail, once again at the foot of a steep, uphill climb. As you face the challenge ahead, what is going through your mind? If you are thinking "Ugh. I should have trained more," then you are thinking of the past. Or maybe you are focused on the future: "I am going to be so exhausted after this climb!" But if you are a mindful hiker, you will simply notice what is in front of you in the present moment: the vibrant colors of the trees, the scent of pine filling the air, the taste of cool, fresh water as you sip from your bottle, the feel of the rocky path under your boots, and the sound of leaves rustling with each step. When the trail rises in front of you, you simply see an uphill path, no more, no less.

Being mindful is more than just being aware. It is also about embodying compassion—the desire for all beings to be free from suffering—and not causing anyone or anything harm. Mindfulness is a commitment to kindness, understanding, and the recognition that our actions have consequences. While awareness will lead you to admire the beauty of a unique plant or stone on your path, mindfulness ensures that you leave them undisturbed, recognizing that removing them could disrupt the natural balance and deprive others of the joy of discovery. You will learn more about the practice of compassion in the next chapter, but for now simply understand that you cannot truly practice one without the other.

MINDFULNESS IN PRACTICE

Having a calm mind is *not* a prerequisite for mindfulness—that would be like having to be in shape before you exercise. Nor are you expected to be mindful all of the time; staying in that mindful state of mind is not easy for most of us equipped with a human brain. We tend to wander off to the past, future, or fantasy, more often than not. When you catch yourself, the mindful response is not to judge yourself, but to simply return your attention back to the present again. And again. And again. Each return to mindful awareness is like a muscle being strengthened, helping you cultivate a habit of presence that enriches all aspects of your life. This is the practice. Like all other skills, you practice it, rather than perform.

The beauty of mindfulness lies in the awareness that you are thinking *and* remembering that awareness is much bigger than your thoughts. Think about this: your awareness is able to experience not only thoughts, but sight, smell, taste, touch, and sound. It is able to simultaneously feel the sensation of your feet on the ground and the breeze on your skin and the smell of the forest.

FOCUSING ON THE PHYSICAL

But what do you do when a really big emotion shows up and becomes a barrier to your ability to be present? Rather than tackling it with your mind, which might lead to overthinking, or ignoring it, which only postpones dealing with it, there's a different approach. Focus on the physical sensations that accompany the emotion. This method bypasses the mental stories and directly engages with what you're feeling in your body, allowing for a more immediate and effective way to handle intense emotions without getting overwhelmed by them. Simply focus on what's physically manifesting in your body—this is key. Is your chest tight? Are your hands clenched? Acknowledge these sensations without judgment. This shift in focus allows you to address the emotion directly and in the moment, an alternative to rumination or avoidance.

Being present and mindful can profoundly support us as we navigate the challenging terrain of grief. Just as a mindful hiker observes each step, each breath, and each moment on the trail, we can apply this same awareness to our journey through grief. This approach helps us manage overwhelming emotions by focusing on the present rather than being consumed by past regrets or future anxieties.

Dr Jon Kabat-Zinn, renowned mindfulness meditation teacher, author, and the creator of Mindfulness-based Stress Reduction (MBSR) says, "As long as you are breathing there is more right with you than wrong with you, no matter what is wrong."[12] When everything seems overwhelmingly negative, mindfulness gives you a gentle invitation to widen your view to include not just your struggles, but what is neutral or even going well, too.

KATARINA'S STORY:
FINDING A NEW PATH

Katarina appeared to have everything under control, with a successful career and a boyfriend she loved dearly. Yet, despite her outward success, she struggled internally, grappling with deep-seated traumas and a family history steeped in chaos. "Addiction is in my blood. I was aware of it, from my earliest memories," she explains, a stark reminder of the biological origin of this disease. "When I was seven years old my father got sober. He moved out of our family's house and moved into a sober living home. He took my bed with him, which was a huge waterbed, and my favorite blanket. I have a crystal-clear memory of my bed and blanket in my dad's new room ... and even though he was still alive, I knew I had also lost my dad."

This event set a precedent for future losses, where her own needs were consistently overlooked in the face of larger family crises. Her mother got a roommate, and gave them Katarina's bedroom. This act was not just a physical deprivation but a symbolic removal of comfort and security, deepening her sense of instability. "This is probably one of the first 'dismissed' losses of my life, one that has stayed with me ever since. But I still have that blanket. It's the oldest, most precious thing I have."

As a teenager, Katarina dabbled extensively with drugs to mask her pain, meticulously keeping track of each encounter. "I counted how many times I did each one," she shares, highlighting her methodical approach to her risky behaviors as a means of control. Even when she developed a gambling addiction it was dismissed as her being competitive, and just wanting to win.

"I was the poster child for 'Work Hard, Play Hard.'" Despite drinking a bottle of wine every night after work, she maintained a semblance of control, never partaking in the morning or losing a job due to her habits. Despite her go-getter facade, anxiety and stress churned on the inside. "I was never good at dealing with feelings. Lucky for me, it wasn't too hard to escape them ... and there were so many other people escaping with me, that even addiction could feel completely normal and even healthy at times," Katarina explained. "I created a side of me that was fearless, full of adventure, FUN ... the party never ended with me ... I was 'happy.' I was free. The weight of my responsibilities, the disappointments in life, the feelings about Whatever, they just went away ... until the morning."

As her life spiraled, Katarina realized she needed a change. "Once I got sober, I lost The Escape. Losing The Escape is like being surrounded by a million knives, pointed right at the edge of your skin. And there's nothing you can do about it. This is how it feels in the beginning. And why so many people go right back to what they were doing. And why the people who don't are the strongest people in the entire world." Her life as she knew it evaporated along with the coping mechanisms she'd relied on to numb the pain, thrusting her into a harsh new reality.

"The life that you knew is Gone. The ways that you had coped with every little thing, from the time you were young, are Gone. All of a sudden you are in this new world with no protection, and you are so sensitive it's as if you no longer have skin. The people you have harmed in some way think you deserve this and don't you dare complain about it—it's all your fault. The people who loved the fun party girl—who may or may not have the same issues as you—do not support this change at all. 'You are boring now.' 'Why would you do this?' 'It makes no sense.' 'You'll be back.'"

"I knew for myself that there was no way I could succeed if I didn't find a new way to deal with stress. Falling apart was not an option and running away to 'get better' wasn't either. And so, I found mindfulness." In her second month of sobriety, Katarina began exploring meditation and was drawn to Buddhist teachings of mindfulness, and yin yoga and restorative yoga, which contrasted with her previous use of yoga purely as exercise. She explained, "Everyone experiences sobriety differently. There is not just one path. For me, I found the mindfulness path to be the most impactful. There are Buddhist recovery groups, there are lots of tattooed sober Buddhist teachers. I found people I could relate to and jumped in wholeheartedly."

Learning to slow down and pay attention—one of the tenets of mindfulness—wasn't easy for her, but this became a crucial part of her routine. She describes her new ritual as "Yoga, and then Tea": "I would walk in the door from work and go straight to my back room—coat on and everything—passing the kitchen where I would normally pour a glass of wine first thing. I would change my clothes and do yoga to release the stress of the day. I wouldn't come out of that room until I had calmed down."

For Katarina, getting sober meant she had to confront her mistakes, and make peace with all the actions she had taken. She also made the very hard choice to sever ties with nearly everyone from her past. "I had no interest in making the old life into a sober one. It would have been miserable," she reflected. "So, no more going out. No more dinners. No happy hour. No social gatherings. No anything. It was work, and then trying to relax."

Even with self-acceptance and sobriety, Katarina acknowledges the nonfinite loss of her old self and her ability to be truly understood by people who have not had to overcome addiction. "You lose a certain ease in relating to others. It can be very lonely if you don't make efforts to connect with other sober people. Because when you're triggered and need extra support, non-sober people don't really understand the extent of the need, and when you're in a state of needing it, it's too hard to explain it. Because All Of This is generally not talked about in our society. And even now, when things are definitely changing, there is still an automatic impulse to be silent and hide the struggle."

Initially, she wasn't alone in her journey; her partner was also embracing sobriety, and together they attended a sobriety group on weekends. But when that relationship ended, she found solace in meditation and yoga classes within a small, supportive community of women. She credits the practices she learned during that period of her life with helping her to not only stay sober, but also to repair the relationship with her father when he was diagnosed with a life-limiting illness.

"When my dad died, I felt like I had somehow joined this club that I didn't even know existed—the 'I have lost a parent' club. There was immediate connection with anyone I came across who had also lost a parent. It's exactly the same with sobriety—but the club isn't as big, as it's not talked about as openly."

Each day, Katarina continues to build on her sobriety, supported by the collective strength of a community that shares her commitment to a sober life. "When you've gotten to the point where you can trust yourself a little, and you're able to take a breath and look out the window, it can be confusing. You know that what you're doing is the right thing. You know that you are healthier, you are learning to take care of yourself, you are learning to Be Awake ... but everyone else seems to be having so much fun, and you aren't allowed anymore. Even now, I sometimes miss the fearless party girl that I used to be. It doesn't matter that the happiness wasn't real and I didn't remember half of what I did. She was a big part of me, and I lost her ... The truth is, I really liked that girl—what I imagined her to be at least."

Katarina still turns to mindfulness to stay grounded. Each day, instead of being swallowed by the narratives of her past life or fears about her future, she focuses on her immediate experiences—the breath in meditation, the stretch in yoga, the calm of the present moment. This mindfulness practice does not erase her challenges, but is a framework that helps her live with them without needing to escape back to alcohol, and has transformed her addiction into a path of personal growth and self-discovery.

PRACTICE:
COMING TO YOUR SENSES

The idiom "coming to your senses" means thinking logically or seeing a situation more clearly. This is precisely the goal of mindfulness, which literally harnesses your senses to bring you clarity in the present moment.

When you notice that you are time traveling, fantasizing, ruminating, or doing anything other than observing the present moment, draw your attention to what you hear, see, taste, smell, and feel. As with all practices, the key to coming to your senses is to notice when you have wandered away from the objective truth and begin again.

Remember, the goal isn't to empty your mind or achieve perfect tranquility but to practice returning to the present moment each time you drift away. Like any skill, mindfulness improves with practice, helping you find calm and clarity in the daily rush of life.

PREPARE FOR PRACTICE

1. Find a quiet place where you can sit undisturbed for a few minutes. You can sit on a cushion on the floor or in a chair. Ensure your posture is supportive and alert, yet relaxed, not stiff or rigid.

2. If you're comfortable doing so, close your eyes. Otherwise, find a neutral point in the space in front of you to softly gaze upon.

SET YOUR INTENTION

3. Take a moment to pause and reflect on what you want to receive from this meditation session. This could be clarity, peace, or simply a break from your day. Tuck this intention away gently in your mind.

FOCUS ON YOUR BREATH

4. Bring your attention to your breath. Feel its natural rhythm as it flows in and out of your body. Try to witness your breath as if it's the very first time you're experiencing it. Notice the sensations of the air entering your nostrils, filling your lungs, and then leaving your body.

ENGAGE YOUR SENSES

5. Begin to broaden your awareness to include the physical sensations throughout your body. Notice how your chest or abdomen rises and falls with each breath. Feel any sensations of warmth, coolness, or air moving across your skin.

6. Gradually shift your focus to sounds. Allow sounds to come to you naturally without seeking them out. Observe how each sound is received by your ears and how it resonates within you.

OBSERVE THOUGHTS AND SENSATIONS

7. As you notice each sensation, thought, or emotion, gently label it to enhance awareness. Use simple tags such as "hearing," "smelling," or "thinking." This helps in acknowledging and distancing yourself from becoming overly attached to these experiences.

8. Additionally, classify these experiences as pleasurable, unpleasurable, or neutral. This practice guides you to observe your reactions more objectively, facilitating a balanced emotional response regardless of the nature of stimuli.

PRACTICE NON-ATTACHMENT

9. Allow your awareness to be like the sky—vast and open. Thoughts, sensations, and sounds are like clouds or birds passing through it; they come and go.

10. If you find yourself getting hooked by a particular thought or feeling, acknowledge its presence, and then let it pass. Remind yourself that these are fleeting, and you don't need to hold on or push them away.

CONCLUDE THE PRACTICE

11. After spending several minutes in this state of awareness, gently bring your attention back to your initial intention. Recognize any differences in how you feel now compared to when you started.

12. Slowly open your eyes (if they are closed) and take a moment to notice your surroundings before getting up.

CHAPTER 6

NAVIGATING THE EMOTIONAL LANDSCAPE WITH COMPASSION

HEARTACHE AND AWE

Many of us experience self-criticism when facing an unwelcome change—cycling between guilt and shame, or enduring self-blame to avoid facing the real pain of what happened. Whatever the reason, self-criticism only deepens your suffering. The path to healing lies in self-compassion: embracing kindness and understanding toward yourself.

My favorite part of being a grief professional is working directly with clients, either in a private session or within my online group. When we first meet, I ask them what inspired them to schedule a session with me or join the group. More often than not, they begin by telling me everything they are doing wrong. They either feel or have been told that they should be stronger, more in control of their emotions. They are not adapting to changes quickly enough or should be further along in their grieving process.

They feel ashamed of what seem like conflicting emotions; the relief and despair after a divorce, or when a loved one dies after a long-term illness. Around the holidays there are always a few people that feel like they should be more excited about the season, but they don't even feel like getting out of bed, much less shopping and going to parties. So many "shoulds."

Then I ask them to tell me their story. They revisit the shock of discovering their partner's affair, a revelation that upended their sense of trust and destroyed their vision of the future. They recount the day they were fired from a job they had poured years of their life into, stripping them of their identity, workplace friends, and finances. They describe the demanding routine of caring for an aging parent with a declining health condition, a role that consumes their time, money, physical and emotional energy. They share how their child who is suffering with an opioid addiction has been missing for months. All a stark contrast to the expected seasonal joy.

And there I sit, with heartache and awe. Being human is really hard. Yet here they are, vulnerable enough to share with me their deepest struggles, not realizing yet that just by showing up for help they are demonstrating a powerful act of self-compassion. Each person's story illuminates more than the pain of loss; it speaks to the incredible resilience they muster without even realizing it. This strength is not chosen; it is forged in the crucible of their unchosen experiences.

When I listen to stories filled with self-doubt and burdened by "shoulds," I am reminded of the transformative power of self-compassion. This practice is not merely helpful, it's essential— the most effective tool we have to soothe and bear the inevitable pain of being human. Yet, for many—including myself at one point—cultivating self-compassion may seem impossible, especially when your hopes are shattered and your world is falling apart. However, it's precisely in these moments that self-compassion is most useful. Time and again, I witness how it gets people through pain that cannot be changed. It can be learned, and for the majority of my clients and myself, embracing self-compassion has been the springboard for hope and self-trust.

THE THREE COMPONENTS OF SELF-COMPASSION

For those of us who identify as chronically self-critical, the very idea of self-compassion may seem ridiculous. The world often reinforces this harsh self-view and negative thought patterns. But by letting go of that self-critical label and turning inward with kindness, rather than self-abandonment, we can begin to give ourselves the care we truly need. Through self-compassion we learn that we deserve the same care and forgiveness we readily extend to others. Self-compassion researchers Dr Kristin Neff and Dr Chris Germer deconstruct this often intimidating concept into three digestible components: mindfulness, common humanity, and self-kindness.

- **Mindfulness** involves maintaining a balanced awareness of our present emotions, and observing them without judgment. To cultivate mindfulness, practice being fully present with your emotions, recognizing and accepting them as they are without trying to change them. This prevents us from being overwhelmed by intense feelings and helps regulate our response to stress.

- **Common humanity** recognizes that suffering and personal failings are universal human experiences, not isolated incidents unique to us. Cultivating a sense of common humanity helps us see that we are part of something larger, alleviating feelings of isolation and loneliness.

- **Self-kindness** is treating ourselves with the same care and understanding as we would a good friend. It involves challenging the critical inner voice that exacerbates our struggles and offering ourselves kindness, understanding, and forgiveness instead.

THE POWER OF HONESTY AND COMPASSION

Emily and Tom had been entwined in a deeply personal and emotionally fraught journey to conceive a child through IVF for over four years. The path was lined with hope, but also shadowed by the immense pressures and uncertainties of fertility treatments. In their third round of IVF, which they financed with the last of Emily's inheritance, the stakes felt higher than ever.

Each morning, Emily would steep a cup of tea and settle onto the couch by the window, gazing out at the yard where she hoped her future child would one day play. Here, in this quiet corner, she tried to nurture a positive future through visualization. "I would close my eyes and imagine being pregnant, feeling the strong, reassuring arms of Tom around me," Emily recalled. Her initial journal entries mirrored these sessions of hopeful imagery—filled with positive affirmations and dreams of nurseries.

However, beneath the surface of these optimistic entries, a storm of unexpressed emotions brewed. Despite the hopeful words she penned, each IVF appointment and test was a battle against a swell of anxiety that she masked with a smile. "I believed being positive would help our chances, but beneath the words, the fear always lingered. I was faking it," Emily revealed.

When she shared this with her therapist, Emily was introduced to the concept of self-compassion. "It was hard to imagine having compassion for myself. I felt like I was doing everything wrong. I wasn't being positive like I was supposed to be. I wasn't getting pregnant like I wanted. But then my therapist shared that self-compassion isn't about being good. It is about being kind." Emily's therapist introduced her to the three components of self-compassion.

The first week focused on mindfulness. Emily practiced just "sitting with" her emotions, observing them without judgment. "My therapist guided me through the process of being present with my anxiety or overwhelm. Well, those feelings would show up, but she told me to just notice how they felt in my body while also breathing. What used to be like overwhelming anxiety felt like a tight throbbing knot in my belly," Emily shared. "But instead of thinking about why I felt this way, or trying to stop it, I just hung out with the feeling until it melted away."

This practice helped her develop a balanced awareness, reducing the intensity of her emotional responses. She began to use this in her journaling too, acknowledging every emotion as it surfaced—anger, sadness, fear—without the compulsion to steer them toward forced positivity. "Writing my real feelings made them seem less overwhelming. I started to feel more genuinely positive because I was no longer suppressing the negative," she shared. This honest acknowledgment of her emotional landscape brought unexpected relief and clarity. Emily described the experience as freeing: "My body and I finally started to understand each other, because I wasn't hiding behind a facade of relentless positivity."

The following week she was introduced to the second component of self-compassion, common humanity. Emily's therapist encouraged her to consider the experiences of others undergoing IVF. "She asked me to reflect on how I viewed others in similar situations. Were they defective? Alone? Bad at getting pregnant? Of course not! Then she asked me to imagine seeing myself through their eyes. And then I got it. My struggle is part of a shared human experience that happens to other women doing IVF. It is not personal failure," Emily explained. "I had to remind myself of this over and over again, but eventually it got easier to remember that I am not the only one going through this."

Self-kindness was the focus in subsequent sessions and continued to be a key element of their work together. Emily learned to treat herself with the same compassion and understanding she would offer a good friend, or other women struggling with infertility. "This one was the hardest for me. Being kind to myself is not something I am used to. But it has been a real shift in my life. I've learned to speak to myself with love and encouragement more often than I used to. I am not perfect at it, but I can be self-compassionate about that too."

One evening, Emily decided to share what she was learning with Tom. She had initially feared what his reaction would be when she told him how hard it was to stay positive, and was surprised when he expressed relief. "It turns out he was faking it a lot too. And hearing how I really felt made him feel closer to me. And ultimately it made us both more hopeful." Their conversation marked a turning point, deepening their relationship through shared vulnerability.

Reflecting on her experience, Emily noted, "Self-compassion hasn't changed how badly I want this baby, but it has changed how I cope with the anxiety, and how I treat myself when things get rough. I have the best partner—and the best me—to face this with, whatever the outcome." Through mindfulness she learned to manage her emotional responses more healthily. Through recognizing her common humanity, she felt less isolated and more connected to others. And through self-kindness she developed a supportive and forgiving relationship with herself, which was crucial for her emotional and mental health. Each of these attitudes not only helped Emily cope with the difficulties of IVF but also enriched her relationship with Tom, illustrating the profound impact self-compassion can have on our lives.

TRANSFORMING SUFFERING TO HOPE

Integrating the three components of self-compassion into daily life can profoundly change how we experience and react to pain. We encourage a more compassionate self-dialogue, greater emotional resilience, and a deeper connection with others—transforming our relationship with ourselves and the world around us. Ultimately, it gives us hope.

The journey of self-compassion is both personal and universal, weaving individual stories into a larger narrative of human vulnerability and strength. As we practice these principles, we not only facilitate our healing but also contribute to a global movement toward greater empathy and understanding.

To truly live with self-compassion, we must continually practice its principles in everyday situations. This might involve pausing to breathe deeply and acknowledge our feelings during a stressful event, reminding ourselves of our common humanity when we notice feelings of isolation, or actively replacing self-criticism with kinder, more supportive self-talk.

These moments of self-compassion can build on one another, creating a life more resilient to stress and more open to joy. They enable us to approach life's challenges with confidence and grace, secure in the knowledge that we are enough, just as we are, and that we are connected in our humanity with others around the world.

Imagine, then, what it would be like to free yourself from this extra blame and shame. Consider the energy that could be reclaimed and redirected toward healing what truly hurts. This isn't about denying the pain or the reality of the situation, but rather about giving yourself permission to face these challenges without the additional internal conflict. By cultivating self-compassion, you create space to breathe, to heal, and to find resilience amid adversity. This approach doesn't change the facts of your situation, but it can significantly alter your experience of it, reducing suffering and facilitating a more compassionate self-awareness.

BEFRIENDING COMPASSION

In this practice, we'll explore self-compassion through a meditation that helps bridge the gap between extending kindness to others and offering the same compassion to ourselves. By visualizing a scenario where we comfort a friend and then applying that same kindness to ourselves, we can deepen our understanding and acceptance of our own emotions.

Following the meditation, it can be beneficial to engage in a journaling exercise to reflect on the experience and solidify the insights gained.

PREPARE YOUR SPACE

1. Find a quiet and comfortable place where you won't be disturbed. You might choose to lie down with supports under your knees and head, sit back in a comfortable chair, or adopt a meditative posture.

2. Spend a few moments settling in, adjusting your position to ensure maximum comfort. Ask yourself, "What does my body need at this moment?" and make any necessary adjustments.

FOCUS ON BREATHING AND RELAXATION

3. Close your eyes and turn your attention to your breath. Begin to slow your breathing in a way that feels comfortable—no need to force it.

4. With each exhale, consciously relax tension in your body—your jaw, shoulders, and belly. Allow yourself to feel supported by the ground or chair, with nowhere to go and nothing to do but breathe.

VISUALIZE COMPASSION

5. Visualize someone, either real or imagined, who is experiencing a challenge similar to yours. Picture them clearly in your mind's eye.

6. Imagine sitting beside this person, feeling a deep sense of empathy for their situation. Reflect on your sincere desire for their relief from suffering, acknowledging that while you cannot change their situation, your presence and understanding can offer comfort.

7. Consider silently or in whispers what you might say or do to express your care and concern. How would you listen to their story without judgment, allowing them to express their emotions freely?

OFFER KINDNESS

8. Think about how you would respond with words of comfort, not advice, emphasizing love, care, and gentleness. Imagine how they might feel after being heard and understood.

REVERSE ROLES

9. Now, imagine that you are the one receiving this kindness and empathy from the other person. Place your hands on your heart or another comforting spot on your body. Feel the warmth and care being offered to you.

10. Take deep, expansive breaths, focusing on feeling the comfort envelop you.

CLOSE THE PRACTICE

11. Offer yourself some words of comfort, encouragement, and understanding. Set an intention to carry this self-compassionate attitude with you throughout your day.

JOURNALING

After the meditation, take some time to journal about your experience. Here are some prompts to guide your reflection:

1. Reflect on giving compassion:

- What emotions did you feel while offering compassion to the imagined person?

- How did it feel to listen and respond to them without judgment?

2. Reflect on receiving compassion:

- How did it feel to imagine receiving kindness and empathy from another?

- What specific words or gestures provided the most comfort?

3. Reflect on insights gained:

- What did you learn about your own needs for compassion and understanding?

- How can you apply this practice of self-compassion to daily situations, especially during challenging times?

CHAPTER 7

WRITING YOUR STORY

WHY KEEP A JOURNAL?

Emotions are often described in metaphorical terms: a roller coaster, a tidal wave, a raging storm, the ground falling out from underneath your feet. Whether you are grappling with the perpetual adjustment demanded by nonfinite losses like chronic illness and caregiving or facing the sharp reality of finite losses such as the death of a loved one, the destruction of your home, or any other major life change, the chaos impacts every part of your being, including your ability to think straight.

You are probably all too familiar with the cognitive challenges of grief. Your mind is foggy, disoriented, and basic decisions like what to have for breakfast or which shoes to wear feel insurmountable. Memory loss is not uncommon, and with that, missed appointments, forgotten dry cleaning, and safety hazards like leaving your house with the stove still turned on.

For most people this mental haze clears over time, but before that happens it is incredibly hard to make sense of what you are feeling, let alone know what it is you need. This is where journaling can help you out, not merely for recording events, but to help you clarify your internal narrative, identify the essence of your feelings, and start to untangle the pile of beliefs, thoughts, and emotions.

If your loss is an ongoing saga without a clear endpoint, such as caring for a loved one, living with a chronic illness, or navigating the unpredictable waters of addiction or mental health challenges, journaling can be a regular check-in that helps you reset your self-care goals day after day. In the struggle with challenges that ebb and flow, the regular practice of journaling can give you stability as you confront the unpredictable. It is also the place where you can voice frustrations, express your outrage, celebrate small victories, and gradually discern patterns in the chaos—revealing insights that help you move forward with resilience.

For other types of loss, such as the death of a loved one, break-up, or divorce, journaling acts as a sanctuary for your thoughts and memories. It allows you to honor what you have lost and articulate your pain, helping you to grapple with your new reality. Writing becomes a ritual of remembrance and adaptation, helping to preserve the connection to your past while helping you rebuild your assumptive world.

I encourage my clients (and myself) to review their journals from time to time. Every three months is a good starting point, but looking back over six months or a whole year will reveal how challenges were navigated, skills were built, and illuminate the growth, that much like a plant growing, is impossible to see in real-time. Your journal entries highlight both your struggles and triumphs, revealing your unique narrative of resilience and adaptability. Writing down your experiences not only captures your truth but can also serve as a valuable reference if you later find yourself or someone else questioning your reality.

MY STORY:
THE HEALING POWER OF WRITING

In tenth grade I was required to write three pages in a single-spaced spiral-bound notebook five days a week for a whole term. This was my introduction to journaling. At first this assignment felt like just another tedious task on my to-do list that I used as an emotional dumping ground for the jumble of complaints, frustrations, fears, crushes, heartaches, and teenaged angst. And while I enjoyed writing book reviews and term papers, the freedom from the rules of spelling and grammar was liberating. I think it was about halfway through my first notebook when I started to go deeper, surprising myself with entries about my Uncle Doug, who died by suicide when I was seven years old. Without prying eyes, I felt safe to explore my unanswered questions around suicide, the afterlife, and the speculations around why he died.

What started as an emotional dumping ground—a place to unload the jumble of teenage feelings about daily frustrations, dreams, and heartaches—became less about rumination and helped me see myself as an individual distinct from my parents, rather than just an extension of their expectations and beliefs. This process, known as individuation, allowed me to recognize and explore my own thoughts and feelings. Through journaling, I learned to slow down and pay attention to my inner patterns, gaining insights even when I was uncertain about how to proceed. This shift led to a gradual understanding that my "past self" was revealing patterns and truths to my "present self." Through my journal I gained the clarity and validation that my experiences were real and persistent, especially those I was trying to dismiss.

One of the most significant applications of my journaling was in dealing with the strained relationship with my father. Over the years, our interactions had been marked by complexity and strain, often leaving me questioning my perceptions and feelings. I do not want to paint the relationship as all bad, but it was not all good, either.

When I was around the age of 19, and after my parents were divorced, my father moved in with his girlfriend and her two high school-aged daughters, explaining that "Those girls don't have a good father like you do. They need me more than you." These were soul-crushing words to my only child ears. Although he would return home from time to time, for the most part I lived alone in the house I grew up in. While I did not mind the freedom (yes, I threw a few wild parties), I felt unmoored, trapped between being a child and becoming an adult, and unsure of the role I was expected to play in my father's new family. I would go to his house to visit, but I always felt like an intruder.

Once they married, my father and his second wife moved back into the house, and I moved out. I was still expected to show up for family gatherings, but I was always anxious and on edge. "You have a nervous laugh," he once told me. "Anyone else tell you that?" Embarrassed, I asked around. My best friends assured me that I had a lovely laugh, and suggested that it was my father's presence that made me tense and changed my demeanor.

Eventually they sold the house and moved several states away to Florida. When I first visited their new home, I noticed that their walls displayed countless photos of her daughters' lives, but not a single one of me. As I moved through the rooms, surrounded by their memories, their closeness, I felt more like an outsider than ever, and spent the next decade trying to avoid them at any cost.

When his wife asked for a divorce, my father rushed back into my life, even writing an apology and asking for a fresh start. I was elated, and for a time we were closer than ever. Even though he talked about his ex-wife and her daughters in a way that made me feel like he would rather have them back than our relationship be repaired, I convinced myself things would get better. When he married his third wife, a warm and lovely human being, I felt like the second family would be put to rest, and everything would be okay again.

But it wasn't. In the prologue to this book, I mentioned a particularly chaotic visit being our downfall. My father rarely came to Maryland to visit me. One winter he called to schedule a trip to see me. He casually mentioned that he would also be visiting the second family to watch his grandson play in a tournament. He gave me the dates that he wanted to spend with me, and I scheduled the classes and private clients at my meditation center accordingly.

Then it snowed. A lot. Enough to reschedule the tournament that the grandson was in, which now landed on the nights we had scheduled to spend time together. My father proposed that we go to dinner on an alternate night, but I had class and clients. I politely told him that I had already rearranged my schedule once, but that I would be happy to spend some quality time with him and eat dinner at home on the couch when I got home that night at 9 PM.

My father was not at my house when I got home at 9 PM. He wasn't home at 10 PM. 11 PM. 12 AM. Panic had long set in. His phone was going to voicemail. Was he dead? Was he with his second wife? Where was he? At 3 AM a voicemail popped up on my phone, and a slurry voice that sounded a bit like my dad said something about drinking too much and staying in a hotel near where the second family lived. I told my husband to go to the kitchen and get the cookies my father had brought with him. I binged them all while screaming angrily between each bite.

My father could never let go of that second family. Nor could he make me a priority. I found out the next day that he hadn't been with the second family that night, but had gone to a happy hour with some former co-workers and had, as the saying goes, one too many.

What does this have to do with journaling? Everything. I have been journaling on and off since the tenth grade. I still have many of them hidden away. The physical act of writing with a pen or pencil on paper helps the writer retain information. This is why I can remember scenarios so clearly now (and it is worth mentioning that I am leaving a lot of what I remember out for brevity). My journals are also time capsules, and I can dig them up as evidence whenever I feel the disorienting fog of being gaslighted, which happened a lot. And reading back as an adult what I experienced as a child gives me so much compassion for myself. Until that tumultuous visit, it was implied that everything was my fault. I can now see that I was just a child trying to get her daddy to meet her needs, and that was something he just could not do.

WRITING TO REBUILD YOUR WORLD

The journaling technique I learned in tenth grade was freewriting, also known as stream of consciousness journaling, where you simply let your thoughts flow onto the page without worrying about grammar, structure, or even coherence. However, if you find yourself ruminating, or stuck in a negative cycle, this method might not be the most helpful. Research by psychologist Dr Wendy Lichtenthal suggests that more structured journaling can significantly improve adaptation to life during or after loss,[13] and her research influenced my guided journal, *From Grief to Peace*.

Writing to explore what this loss means to you, or its greater significance, can facilitate a better adjustment. The technique includes exploring different explanations for the loss, why it matters, and recognizing that your interpretations can evolve over time. Additionally, directed writing tasks can help create distance from overwhelming thoughts and enable a more structured reflection that aligns with your belief system and values. If you are further along in navigating your grief, writing about how the loss has led to meaningful changes in life goals or values can be particularly therapeutic.

Grief therapist Robert Neimeyer explains that grieving is a dynamic process of reconstructing meaning in a world that has been fundamentally altered by loss. We naturally strive to make sense of our losses by integrating our experiences meaningfully into our ongoing life stories. This process, known as meaning reconstruction, is not about finding a way to move on from the grief as if it never happened, but rather about finding a way to live with it in a manner that acknowledges the pain while simultaneously making space for personal growth and future possibilities. We are either compelled to assimilate this new reality into our existing beliefs, or to fundamentally change our understanding of the world to accommodate this new, painful truth.

Journaling is a powerful ally in this process. By writing about your loss, you engage actively in narrative retelling—putting into words the story of what you have lost and how it affects you. This can help you process and organize your thoughts and feelings, providing a clearer sense of how the loss has reshaped your identity and life.

Neimeyer suggests that this type of writing helps move you from a place of chaos to one of coherence. The narrative you create through journaling helps reconstruct your personal story, incorporating the loss into a new understanding of who you are and how you relate to the world. This doesn't mean the pain goes away, but it can become more manageable and integrated into your life.[14]

- **Express all emotions**: Start by writing down whatever comes to mind about the loss. Don't hold back. It's important to acknowledge all feelings—sadness, anger, confusion, or even relief—without judgment. This unfiltered expression can be a relief in itself.

- **Recount memories**: Write about your memories with the person or situation you've lost. This can include happy times, challenging times, or mundane moments. Recalling these memories can help you see the role they played in your life and can bring a sense of peace and gratitude amid the pain.

- **Reflect on impact**: Consider how the loss has changed you. Has it altered your view of the world? Your understanding of yourself? Writing about these changes can help you see how you've grown and what strengths you've drawn on or developed.

- **Imagine conversations**: Sometimes, you might have things left unsaid. Through journaling, you can write out these conversations. This can be a way to say goodbye, to express love, or to voice regrets and forgiveness.

- **Find new meanings**: As you write, you might discover new insights or connections that help you find meaning in the loss. This doesn't mean justifying what happened, but finding a way to live with it that acknowledges the pain but also the possibilities for the future.

TIPS FOR JOURNALING

Journaling is a blend of content and process. The content encompasses the ideas, emotions, and information you wish to communicate, forming the substance of your writing. Whether you're journaling about personal experiences, crafting a narrative, or arguing a point, the content is what you are sharing with your audience. Meanwhile, the process involves the act of journaling itself. Understanding and honing both the content and the process are crucial for creating impactful, meaningful writing that deepens your relationship with yourself.

Remember, journaling is a personal and flexible process. There are no right or wrong ways to do it. The key is to keep writing, exploring, and being open to where your thoughts lead you. Over time, this practice can offer you a way to live with loss that feels more bearable and meaningful, helping pave the way for healing and growth.

- **Keep writing**: Aim to keep your pen moving or your fingers typing without pausing too much. This continuous flow of writing helps bypass the critical mind and allows deeper insights and emotions to surface.

- **Ignore spelling and grammar**: Don't worry about spelling mistakes, grammatical errors, or sentence structure. The goal is to capture your thoughts and feelings as they come, without the interruption of correcting errors.

- **Set a timer**: If you find it hard to keep writing, try setting a timer. Start with five or ten minutes and write continuously until the timer goes off. This can help build a habit and ease the pressure of feeling like you need to write for a long time.

- **Use evocative music**: Playing music that resonates with your mood or the topic you're writing about can help evoke emotions and memories, enriching your writing experience.

- **Write without judgment**: Approach your journaling with an attitude of non-judgment. This is your private space to express yourself freely. Allow whatever needs to come out without critiquing it for value, importance, or emotional weight.

- **Avoid editing as you go**: Resist the urge to go back and edit your work while you are writing. The editing process can inhibit the flow of thoughts and feelings. There will always be time to refine your entries later if you choose.

- **Choose a comfortable space**: Find a quiet and comfortable place where you feel secure and undisturbed. Comfort in your physical environment can help you open up more deeply in your writing.

- **Regular practice**: Try to journal regularly. Whether daily, weekly, or as needed, consistency helps develop depth in your reflections.

- **Explore different mediums**: If words feel limiting, remember that journaling can also include sketches, collages, or other visual elements. This can be especially useful when emotions are difficult to articulate with words alone.

PRACTICE:
REVISITING A FAMILIAR STORY IN A NEW LIGHT

In this practice, you are invited to revisit a familiar narrative in your life, a story you've often repeated. This story may define a part of who you are or may have significantly shaped your perspective. By approaching this narrative with fresh eyes and new tools, you have the opportunity to transform how you relate to it to uncover deeper insights or discover altered meanings. Exploring a well-told story from different angles can illuminate hidden layers and provide a richer understanding of your experiences.

Below, several creative techniques are offered for you to employ. You may choose one or combine several to enrich your exploration. By engaging with your story creatively, you give yourself a chance to understand it more deeply and perhaps even let go of parts that no longer serve you.

WRITE WITH YOUR NON-DOMINANT HAND

Think of a story that you often recount. Now, take a pen in your non-dominant hand and start rewriting this story. It might feel awkward and slow, but that's the point. This method can engage different parts of your brain, possibly bringing forth new insights or emotions about the story. What feels different when you write it this way? Do any new details or emotions emerge?

COLOR YOUR DIALOGUES

Choose different colored pens for different voices within your narrative. You might use one color for your current self, another for your past self, and a third for another person involved in the story. Write a dialogue between these voices. What would your current self say to your past self? How might the other person in your story respond? This technique can help you explore the different perspectives and perhaps resolve old conflicts or misunderstandings.

DETAIL YOUR THOUGHTS

Dive deep into the details of your story. Describe every aspect with intense detail—the colors, the sounds, the smells, and the textures. How do your detailed descriptions affect the emotional landscape of the story? Does focusing on the details change your understanding or feelings about what happened?

USE VISUAL ELEMENTS

If words feel inadequate or you just want to explore a different medium, try drawing, making a collage, or creating a storyboard of your story. Use whatever materials you have—pencils, paints, magazines, etc. Focus on conveying the emotions and dynamics of the story through visuals. What do you notice about the story when you see it illustrated? Do the visuals bring out aspects of the story that are usually overlooked?

BREAK THE RULES

Write your story without any concern for grammar, spelling, or punctuation. Feel free to misspell words, create new words, and ignore punctuation rules. This can be incredibly freeing and might allow you to express rawer, more genuine emotions. How does the story change when you write without restrictions? What emotions or ideas come out that are usually restrained?

ROTATE YOUR PERSPECTIVE

Literally turn your journal sideways or upside down and write your story from this new angle. Your mental perspective might mirror this shift in your physical perspective, helping you see elements of your story in a different light.

REFLECT

After you have completed your chosen exercises, take a moment to reflect on the experience. How did these creative approaches affect your view of the story? Did they bring out new themes or details that you hadn't considered before? Write a few sentences about what you learned from this practice.

CHAPTER 8

BUILDING RESILIENCE THROUGH RITUAL

THE MILE MARKERS
OF YOUR LIFE

When I first start hiking my local trail and my legs are fresh, I barely notice the mile markers as I pass them by. But toward the end, as my energy wanes and each step takes more effort than the last, the same mile markers become beacons of reassurance. Mile after mile, they remind me just how far I have come, let me know that I am on the right path, and invite me to pause for a moment to rest, so I can gather strength for the journey ahead.

Rituals function in a similar way; they mark a moment in time and space when we pause to acknowledge where we have been and where we want to go. Unlike routine behaviors or habits, which are often automatic and designed to efficiently manage daily tasks, rituals are intentional and imbued with deeper meaning. They are deliberate acts that connect us to our cultural, spiritual, or personal milestones, offering a structured response to life's significant events. They are a scaffolding upon which we can safely express our emotions, acknowledge what matters, and symbolically move from one season of life to another.

Reflect on a meaningful ritual from your life—perhaps a graduation, birthday, wedding, or anniversary—and how it fulfilled your needs, whether personal, social, physical, financial, or spiritual. Think about the emotions stirred, the connections forged, and the memories created by this event. Now, imagine if that day had passed without recognition: no gatherings, no celebrations. The absence of this deliberate marker in time could render the memory of that milestone less vivid, the achievement might feel incomplete, or perhaps even meaningless. Such rituals not only celebrate our milestones but also affirm our identities. Without them, these special moments, whether happy or sad, can feel meaningless. In times of grief, it can further disenfranchise the loss.

JENN AND CONNOR'S STORY:
RITUALS AND CONNECTION

Jenn was a successful entrepreneur, single, and content, living with her cat Connor in a large metropolitan city. Connor was her everything. "He was the one I talked to every day. He was the one I went to bed with every night," she shared. Their profound bond was incomprehensible to those without pets, but Jenn was more than content. He was her confidant, companion, and comfort—a feeling many pet owners know quite well.

Jenn loved Connor as much as he seemed to love her, and when he fell ill, she cared for him with all the love he deserved. Taking him back and forth to the vet, buying him special food, and ensuring he was as comfortable as possible. Jenn was crushed by an overwhelming and inescapable void on the day he died. But she also felt an inexplicable compulsion to write a letter to him. "For whatever reason, it was clear to me that this was what I was supposed to do." That evening, just hours after he died, she wrote her first letter to Connor. Talking to him through her writings felt as natural and comforting as their daily conversations. "Writing to him kept something alive and made me feel a tiny bit less alone," she realized.

Day after day, she kept writing to her beloved cat, and now recognizes this practice as an ongoing ritual that is a cherished part of her routine. During particularly difficult times she writes to him several times a day to help her feel grounded and connected. "I would write to him before turning to any person," she shared, highlighting the depth of their continuing relationship. This practice became Jenn's way of preserving their unique bond, something she felt went beyond any of her human relationships. "There was a connection that was different than anything possible with a person if that makes sense," she explained. "It was so special that it can never be replaced ... and I hold on to it in any way I can."

As Jenn navigated through her grief, she created other rituals to cope with her loss. When she received Connor's ashes, she set up a traditional altar with flowers and a picture. However, she found this inadequate and was surprised that it did not give her the comfort she had hoped it would. "It just wasn't good enough. It didn't feel right," Jenn described her feelings of discomfort. One day, noticing how the sunlight landed on Connor's favorite lounging spot, she placed his ashes there. "For the first time, things felt right," she said. She placed his ashes in all of his favorite spots throughout their home, occasionally moving them with the sun or placing them in her lap or beside her in the bed. "I felt crazy most of the time, but it was comforting to me, so I didn't care," Jenn admitted.

As time passed, Jenn considered adopting new pets. She realized this would mean putting her energy into her new companion animals, and gradually relinquished some of her practices with Connor's ashes. "I knew I had to let go of it in order to move on and have room for new connections," she shared. She made the difficult transition gradually. Initially, she continued to sleep with his ashes and occasionally placed them in her lap. Over time, she did this less frequently, finally putting his ashes in a dedicated spot.

Now with two new cats in her home, Jenn's daily messages to Connor remain constant. "No matter what, I write to him every day. He is present in my life always," she affirmed. This ongoing ritual keeps her connection to Connor alive and active. She admits that she went to great lengths to maintain continuity in her ritual, including spending a good bit of money on specific cat-themed notebooks. When they were discontinued, she panicked. "I ordered the last three from some random store in North Carolina, and hopefully they are really there and get sent to me. If they do, I will have 18 little notebooks, one for each year of his life," she explained. Her ritual illustrates the therapeutic power of maintaining connections after a death, companion animals included. She recognizes now that this practice connects her both to Connor, and to herself.

CREATING YOUR OWN THERAPEUTIC RITUAL

Often, non-death and other disenfranchised losses lack the community support and rituals granted to more recognized losses. Jenn found a technique that helps her validate a grief that is so often disenfranchised by others. A ritual, whether it's a series of actions performed alone or with others, helps you acknowledge the significance of what's been lost. They offer a way to express your emotions and provide a sense of community and support. These can range from funerals and memorial services to less formal acts like journaling or creating art.

When no sanctioned rituals exist for your loss, you have the freedom to create your own, drawing inspiration from religious, spiritual, or cultural traditions, or starting entirely from scratch. The key is to craft a ritual that holds deep personal significance. This could involve writing letters, as Jenn did, creating artwork, hosting a drum circle with people who have experienced a similar loss, or even working with your community to facilitate a public ceremony. The most important aspect is that the ritual resonates with you and helps you navigate your journey of grief or transition.

The first step to creating your own ritual is to set a meaningful intention that honors the event or transition you wish to acknowledge. This act of intention-setting is crucial as it guides everything from the elements to the design and emotional experience you want to evoke. Thanatologist and grief therapist Ken Doka has outlined four types of therapeutic rituals, adaptable to a broad spectrum of needs and situations.[15]

RITUALS OF CONTINUITY

These ongoing rituals signify that something still matters deeply to you— whether it's commemorating a person in your life who has passed away or marking the anniversary of significant personal milestones like the day you became emancipated from an abusive relationship, which could be seen as a rebirth. These rituals could include lighting a candle daily, regularly writing to your loved one as Jenn does with Connor, visiting a significant place regularly, or even celebrating a "re-birthday" every year to acknowledge endurance and renewal.

RITUALS OF TRANSITION

Transition rituals help affirm that you have entered a new phase in your grief journey or life path. For instance, participating in a unique community ceremony, like a ritual at a local queer bar, can mark the acceptance of personal or communal change, helping you and others recognize and adapt to new realities.

RITUALS OF RECONCILIATION

These rituals involve seeking or offering forgiveness, which can be crucial in healing relationships or coming to peace with past events. A ritual could be as simple as writing a letter of forgiveness to someone (sent or unsent) or holding a small ceremony where you verbally release any feelings of resentment or guilt.

RITUALS OF AFFIRMATION

Such rituals are ways to acknowledge legacies or express gratitude. They can involve creating a memorial space that honors a loved one, or perhaps organizing an event that celebrates the contributions of a person or group to your life. Saying thanks through these actions not only keeps memories alive but also strengthens the bonds between you and those you are honoring.

THE FORMAT OF YOUR RITUAL

Each type of ritual, whether private or public, one-time or ongoing, plays a crucial role in the grieving process. They offer different benefits that can help you find your path through sorrow, providing both personal solace and communal support.

PRIVATE VS. PUBLIC RITUALS

Private rituals allow you to engage in deeply personal acts of remembrance and healing, tailored just for you. In the privacy of your own space, you can reflect and process your emotions without the influence or presence of others. This might include writing heartfelt letters to a departed loved one, capturing what you wish you could say to them now. Or perhaps taking solo walks through places that were significant to both of you, where the quiet of nature can offer solace and a sense of connection. Private meditation sessions can also be powerful, providing a space to sit with your feelings and find peace amid the grief. The benefit of private rituals lies in their flexibility to fit your emotional state at any given moment, allowing you to grieve at your own pace and in your own way.

Public rituals, on the other hand, involve your community, offering support and shared healing. These rituals can be incredibly comforting, knowing that you are not alone in your grief. Examples include memorial services where friends and family gather to celebrate the life of the deceased, share stories, and offer comfort to each other. Community prayers can bring collective solace, while public celebrations of life—like a tree planting or charity event in honor of your loved one—create a legacy of love that others can contribute to. The benefit of public rituals is that they reinforce the support network around you, providing strength and consolation through communal presence and shared memories.

Building on this foundation of community involvement, rituals grounded in cultural or religious practices serve as a vital bridge between an individual's inner world and the community's shared beliefs. Each culture and religion has unique ways of marking significant life events, including non-death losses such as transitions, endings, and changes, which are often overlooked. Globally, communities utilize rituals to navigate complex emotions and life changes. In many cultures, rituals that involve the entire community can last for several days, emphasizing collective experiences of grief or celebration.

ONE-TIME VS. ONGOING RITUALS

One-time rituals mark significant moments or anniversaries and serve as formal acknowledgments of your loss. These rituals can provide a sense of closure and a formal way to say goodbye. Scattering ashes in a meaningful place, for example, can be a powerful act of letting go, while also honoring the connection you shared. Holding a memorial service soon after the loss helps to consolidate the community's grief and offers a shared moment to commemorate the life of the loved one. The benefit of one-time rituals is that they help encapsulate the gravity of the loss, allowing you and others to acknowledge it openly and begin the healing process.

Ongoing rituals provide continuous connection and remembrance, helping you incorporate the memory of your loved one into daily life. Lighting a candle every night can serve as a quiet moment of reflection and remembrance. Making weekly visits to a cherished place, such as a park bench dedicated in their name, can feel like a standing appointment with your loved one, keeping their presence alive in your routine. Annual gatherings or remembrance events on significant dates ensure that as time passes, the memory of the loved one evolves with you and your life changes. The benefit of ongoing rituals is that they offer a structured way to continue honoring and remembering your loved one, which can be particularly comforting as you navigate the long-term journey of grief.

SYMBOLIC ELEMENTS

It's crucial to personalize your rituals, transforming generic ceremonies into meaningful expressions of individual grief and celebration. By incorporating elements that are uniquely significant to you, the ritual will resonate more deeply and be more therapeutic.

PRIMAL ELEMENTS

Primal elements tap into ancient symbolic properties, enhancing your connection to the natural world and its cycles. Traditionally, each is connected to a cardinal direction, and has a particular property.

- **Air (North):** Signifies wisdom, freedom, and the mind. Incorporate incense, feathers, or simply the act of deep breathing to connect with clarity and intellect.

- **Earth (South):** Grounds and activates your physical body so you can move through the world in a conscious way. Include crystals, soil, stones, and plants to represent stability and the nourishing aspects of life.

- **Fire (East):** Symbolizes illumination and spirit, releasing darkness and internal struggles so you can move forward and transform into who you want to become. Safely light a candle, or burn written messages in a firepit.

- **Water (West):** Represents emotion and transforms murky feelings into clarity so you can see what was once hidden. Prepare a bowl of water and gaze at the reflection, or cleanse your hands before and after the ceremony with purified water.

SENSORY ELEMENTS

Engaging all your senses helps to create a fully immersive ritual experience. Sensory elements can enhance the emotional and psychological impact of your practice.

- **Sight:** Choose items that are visually striking or meaningful, such as photographs, meaningful decorations, or colorful flowers.

- **Sound:** Integrate music, ringing bells, or natural sounds like waves or wind that resonate with your emotional state or memories.

- **Smell:** Use incense, essential oils, or scented candles to evoke memories or emotions, aiding in relaxation or invigoration.

- **Taste:** Incorporate foods or drinks that are significant to you, whether they are comforting or celebratory.

- **Touch:** Include objects with varied textures that you can hold or feel, such as smooth stones, soft fabrics, or even symbolic tokens.

TEMPORAL ELEMENTS

Temporal elements focus on the timing and phases of your experience, helping to mark the progression from one state of being to another.

- **Before:** Gather items that represent your life and state before the transition or loss. This might include photographs, old letters, or other memorabilia.

- **During:** Choose items that symbolize the process or moment of change itself. This could be a piece of broken glass to signify rupture, a twisted piece of metal, or even a transitional object like a bridge.

- **After:** Select items that reflect the new reality or the lessons learned. These could be symbols of new beginnings, like seeds or an image of a baby bird.

- **Future:** Include items that represent your hopes or goals for what comes next. This could be a blank book, a road map, or a compass.

BECOMING WHO YOU ARE NOW

Recently I went to our local queer night club on a Saturday with a few friends to dance, one of my favorite self-care practices. I spotted an elegant looking woman far across the room. She was wearing a black bodysuit with a long black tutu, accessorized with a crown on her head and a sash that read "Just Divorced." She was accompanied by two "divorcemaids" in equally stunning attire.

Just before midnight, she invited everyone in the club to join her in the outdoor courtyard for a special ceremony. Her designated Master of Ceremonies led a call-and-response style chant, then invited the guest to form a circle around the lady in black. One by one we shouted out our name to signal our willingness to witness her transformation. To the beat of the club music in the background, she danced in the middle of the circle, shed her tutu, and was pronounced by the Master of Ceremonies unmarried and free. We danced around her for a song or two, then walked through her receiving line. As we filed back into the club, she was hugged, congratulated, and offered well wishes by friends and strangers alike.

The stories shared in this chapter, from the vibrant, wild, and communal celebration at the nightclub to the quiet, reflective moments experienced by Jenn, show how each ritual, grand or intimate, serves as a powerful affirmation of one's identity and a bold declaration of personal narrative. By creating a ritual that truly reflects who you are, you honor your experiences, your hardships, and your growth. You will remember this because it matters—because it's a meaningful part of your journey.

PRACTICE:
MARKING LIFE'S UNSEEN MILESTONES

Creating a personal therapeutic ritual can be a powerful way to process and honor significant changes in your life. This exercise will guide you through designing a personal ritual to mark a significant milestone in your journey. Whether you are seeking to acknowledge loss, celebrate a transition, or express gratitude, this ritual can serve as a meaningful and healing practice.

SET YOUR INTENTION

1. Start by setting a clear intention for your ritual. Reflect in your journal on why this ritual is important to you and how it will serve as a significant marker in your life. Choose from one of the following therapeutic intentions:

- Continuity: To remember and honor what has been lost.

- Transition: To celebrate and acknowledge where you are on your journey.

- Reconciliation: To seek or extend forgiveness.

- Affirmation: To recognize a legacy or express gratitude.

CHOOSE YOUR SYMBOLIC ELEMENTS

2. Select items that resonate with your chosen intention. Consider incorporating elements associated with:

- Primal elements: Earth, air, fire, and water, each bringing unique energies to your ritual (see page 93).

- Sensory elements: Sight, sound, smell, taste, and touch, to engage all your senses and enhance the emotional depth of the ritual (see page 94).

- Temporal elements: Symbols representing before, during, after, and future, to reflect on the different stages of your journey (see page 94).

PLAN AND REHEARSE THE RITUAL

3. Rehearse: Before conducting the ritual, plan each step to ensure a smooth flow. Run through the sequence of actions you intend to perform. This preparation helps prevent unexpected interruptions and ensures that each part of the ritual resonates with your intentions.

4. Set the scene: In addition to your symbolic items, you may wish to plan to have music, candles, incense, or other items that contribute to a sacred space.

5. Prepare your space: Create a space where the ritual will take place, either indoors or outdoors. Ensure it is somewhere you feel safe and won't be disturbed. Arrange your chosen items thoughtfully around this space, creating a setting that feels sacred and conducive to introspection and expression.

6. Consider how to open the ceremony: This could be a simple action to signify the beginning, such as lighting a candle or ringing a bell.

7. Plan your ceremony: Decide how you will engage with the symbolic items through actions such as placing stones, pouring water, singing, dancing, or writing a message.

8. Contemplate how you will conclude the ritual: Consider a gesture to symbolically close the ritual, such as extinguishing the candle, gathering the items, or a moment of silence.

9. Reflect on your post-ritual gestures: Decide what to do with the symbolic items ahead of time—whether to keep them, give them away, or respectfully dispose of them in a way that feels fitting for your journey.

CONDUCT YOUR RITUAL

10. With your space set and your plan rehearsed, engage in the ritual. Move through each step with mindfulness, allowing yourself to fully experience the emotional significance of each action. Remember to breathe naturally and stay attuned to your body's responses, adjusting your pace if you find yourself outside your window of tolerance.

CLOSE THE RITUAL

11. Conclude your ritual in whichever way you have chosen. As you gather all the items, reflect on the experience. Tune into any sensations or emotions that have arisen. Verbally or mentally state your closure, such as, "I acknowledge these changes in my life, and I am ready to move forward with strength and awareness."

JOURNALING

If you wish, record in your journal what was particularly meaningful.

CHAPTER 9

REORIENTING TOWARD YOUR FUTURE

FINDING MEANING

Personally, I don't believe that everything happens for a reason. I do believe we often find meaning in what happens.

The idea that when faced with suffering we can find ways to choose how to handle it, find meaning in it, and use that understanding to move forward is captured by holocaust survivor Victor Frankl in his eye-opening book, *Man's Search for Meaning*. He explores how even in the direst circumstances such as the Holocaust, people could still discover a sense of purpose or significance in their struggles. This powerful notion emphasizes that while events may not occur for clear reasons, our response to them can give our lives a meaning that helps us carry on.

I want to be clear that this does not mean that hardship is a gift—it is a challenge that demands much from us, often more than we feel prepared to handle. And yet we can learn new coping skills, practice self-care, and receive insights that were once obscured by the immediacy of loss. This is not a reward for your grief, but the hard-earned wisdom of your dedication to navigating through it with intention.

This wisdom does not usually arise right away, but in looking back over your experience with equanimity—a calm and steady mind—you will likely notice your growing resilience. You may recognize how you have learned to reach out and connect with others for support, or how you have discovered inner strengths you didn't know you had. Perhaps you have honed your ability to adapt to new situations, or found that you can find joy and gratitude in small, everyday moments, despite the pain. These insights often reveal how our struggles can shape us into more compassionate and empathetic individuals, both toward ourselves and others.

Have you ever come across a neatly stacked pile of rocks along a hiking trail? These are cairns, intentionally assembled to serve as markers. Just like trail blazes and mile markers, cairns guide hikers, reassuring them that they are on the right path and helping to navigate through difficult or unclear sections of the trail. Just as these stone markers offer direction and assurance in the wilderness, reflecting on key experiences in our lives can serve a similar purpose. By identifying and mentally grouping your significant moments, you create your own personal cairns, helping you to see how far you have come and preparing you for whatever lies ahead.

The idea of building personal cairns ties into the concept of post-traumatic growth, which is the positive psychological change that occurs as a result of adversity and challenges. This concept, introduced by psychologists Richard Tedeschi and Lawrence Calhoun, highlights five key components:

- **Appreciation of life:** You might find yourself cherishing every moment more deeply after overcoming adversity. Simple joys like a sunrise or a quiet moment with a book may become more precious, offering you a richer, fuller experience of life.

- **Relationships with others:** As you navigate through tough times, you might notice your relationships with family and friends becoming stronger. You might find comfort in connecting with others who have been through similar challenges or appreciate the support of loved ones in new ways.

- **New possibilities in life:** In the wake of hardship, you may see new paths and opportunities that were not apparent before. This could involve changing careers to something that feels more meaningful, or taking up new hobbies that bring joy and satisfaction into your life.

- **Personal strength:** You may discover an inner strength you didn't know you had. Overcoming difficulties often leads you to realize that you are more resilient and capable than you previously thought, equipping you to handle future challenges with greater confidence.

- **Spiritual change:** Your beliefs and sense of spirituality might evolve. You could find yourself questioning old beliefs or deepening your spiritual life as a way to make sense of your experiences and find peace.

The idea of post-traumatic growth does not suggest that you won't experience bitterness or struggle. It means that you can open yourself up to what has changed for the good while missing what is lost. Like meaning reconstruction, discerning these changes may take time—from months to decades.

PATRICE'S STORY.
IT'S OKAY TO TAKE CARE OF ME

Patrice sensed something was amiss when her favorite uncle picked up her and her brother from school. Instead of driving home, they pulled in the driveway of a strange house, where her mother revealed they would be leaving the family farm, and Patrice's unfaithful father, to start anew. Although it was just five miles away from her childhood home, the life 12-year-old Patrice knew was suddenly worlds away.

"Losing my home overnight and having a parent who was not communicative, I was not able to process much of what happened." Wrestling with too many unanswered questions, young Patrice did what children often do when they don't have enough information; she filled in the blanks, developing her own stories in an attempt to make sense of the loss of life as she knew it.

As a young adult, Patrice was fiercely independent, determined to never rely on anyone else. "I earned my own money very early in life and always had a back-up plan." But hyper-independence can bring its own challenges. "I closed a part of myself off and became introverted in a not-so-good way, which may have scared off the few well-meaning people who wanted to help. For many, many years, I felt damaged in a way that surely impacted my decision making and my ability to be resilient. Unsurprisingly, I became depressed."

Patrice went many years without treatment for her depression. When she finally started therapy at the age of 21, she found it so beneficial that she was inspired to become a social worker herself. Once established, she found the work very satisfying, but her savior complex—the continuous need to help others at her own expense—resulted in compassion fatigue and burnout. She recognized that her drive to provide care for others was rooted in a deep need to mend fractured parts within herself.

Eventually, Patrice learned to soften her armor, which allowed her to receive the support she so badly needed. She confided in her friends and found validation and inspiration in books, particularly fiction focused on other people's grief and lost love. She even learned how to self-soothe by practicing yoga, meditation, journaling, and mandala drawing—self-care practices she picked up in her thirties.

"I've learned that it is okay to take care of me and take time for me," Patrice shares, now four decades into her rewarding career as a social worker. She has also made peace with her past, adjusting her view of events from her childhood. She shared that while she feels her parents could have handled the separation with more care and concern for her and her siblings, it was better in the end that they did not stay together.

"I learned that, along with listening to our own inner self, outside support is the absolute key to surviving a deep, deep loss. It is up to us to allow or invite that support into our hearts to ease whatever we are going through. In addition, being able to 'get the pain outside ourselves' is paramount to moving forward with life and the loss in our hearts."

There are many parallels between Patrice's journey and my own. Reflecting on her journey, she shares that, "Looking back, I see the wisdom in my choices—some were textbook reactions, some I regret, but many have shaped me into the person I am proud to be today." Patrice ultimately found a balance between self-reliance, financial security, and belonging to a circle of supportive friends, along with sustainable self-care practices. Like Patrice, I had to learn how to manage distress in a healthy way, and it led to a new career. Remember that new career that was born from my experience at Kripalu? This is the essence of it: sharing what I've learned and helping you cultivate your own healthy coping skills.

MOVING FORWARD
WITH YOUR EXPERIENCE

In Phoenix Rising Yoga Therapy, the style in which I am trained, the most illuminating part of a session is the integration meditation at the end. Integration in this context means exploring how the significant moments of a session either appear or do not appear within your day-to-day life, tapping into your inner wisdom, and creating a small and doable action step that moves you toward your personal goals. I begin by inviting my client to reflect on what felt significant during the session, be it a specific movement, a particular emotion, or a thought. Then they consider if what stood out in the session shows up in their day-to-day life. If it does, do they want more or less of it? If it does not, would they want it to? The final step is supporting them as they identify specific actions they can take to achieve their goal.

This method of integration can be applied to any experience or period in your life, not just during therapy sessions. It can be helpful to do this practice months, years, or even decades down the road. As a young child, there was no way that Patrice could predict how her family's move and her parents' divorce would impact her later in life. However, with the benefit of hindsight, she recognizes how these challenges fostered her personal growth and resilience. Over time, she has come to appreciate the strength developed during those turbulent years. You, too, may not be able to see how your current experiences will shape you. In time, you will look back and understand the ways you have changed—some changes may be positive, others less so—but if you have chosen to meet yourself with compassion and care, you will likely be more resilient to future stress.

Patrice's journey from confusion to a resilient, self-caring adulthood is a perfect example of post-traumatic growth. Despite the very unwelcome change, she cultivated strength and nurtured her relationships, transforming adversity into a foundation for profound personal development. By reflecting on her past, identifying positive changes, and embracing support, Patrice built a more fulfilling life, demonstrating the transformative power of turning hardships into opportunities for growth.

As you navigate your own experiences with grief, look for changes in your life appreciation, shifts in relationships, new opportunities, increases in personal strength, or spiritual developments. These insights are the stepping stones to integrating your experiences and reorienting toward a future that respects both your past and your potential. This approach is about moving forward with grief, leveraging the lessons and strengths gained from adversity for future growth.

Living with loss is a continuous journey—it does not simply end, nor does it need to engulf your life with perpetual sorrow. Grief's presence will fluctuate, sometimes feeling intense and at other times barely noticeable; such variability is a normal part of processing deep emotional connections. To manage this effectively, consider adopting practical strategies like maintaining a routine, participating in support groups, or continuing therapeutic practices like journaling or mindfulness. Being aware of what triggers your grief can also help you handle its ebb and flow more effectively. Incorporating these strategies into your daily life ensures that grief, while a part of your journey, does not overshadow your ability to live fully and meaningfully.

PRACTICE:
REFRAMING LOSS

This guided journaling exercise is a practical tool for reframing loss, a process that involves reinterpreting an event or experience to find a more positive or meaningful perspective. Reframing doesn't diminish the reality of your loss; rather, it helps you see beyond the immediate pain to recognize potential growth and empowerment. By using this approach across the seven domains of life— Physical/Health, Emotions/Feelings, Cognitive/Mental, Relationships, Spiritual/ Religious, Career/Hobbies, and Financial—you can actively shape your journey through grief.

1. **Acknowledge what was lost:** Honor the reality of your experiences by clearly identifying your loss. This step involves recognizing and accepting these changes without judgment.

2. **Identify what was gained:** Open yourself up to the possibility of post-traumatic growth. Notice any new strengths, insights, or shifts in perspective that have emerged from your experiences. Remember, it's completely normal if not every area of life shows apparent gains.

3. **Decide what to create:** Empower yourself by choosing what to build or focus on moving forward. Take control where you can and set intentions that align with your values and the new insights you've gained.

PHYSICAL/HEALTH

- **Lost:** Reflect on any changes in your health or physical abilities. Have you noticed less energy, or perhaps new limitations?

- **Gained:** Think about positive health practices or improvements you've made. Maybe you started walking daily or adjusted your diet.

- **Create:** Set specific goals for improving or maintaining your physical well-being. Plan to join a yoga class or prepare home-cooked meals twice a week.

EMOTIONS/FEELINGS

- **Lost:** Consider the emotional states or expressions that feel diminished. Do you find it harder to feel joy or excitement?

- **Gained:** Identify insights into new emotional strengths or understandings. Perhaps you've discovered a newfound resilience or empathy.

- **Create:** Envision a state of emotional balance or healing. What steps can you take to foster emotional well-being? Maybe establish a routine of journaling or meditation.

COGNITIVE/MENTAL

- **Lost:** Acknowledge notable changes in focus, memory, or mindset. Have you been more forgetful or less able to concentrate?

- **Gained:** Celebrate new knowledge, skills, or perspectives acquired. You might have learned a new language or taken up a skill like photography.

- **Create:** Aim for continued mental growth or shifts in thinking. Set a goal to read one book a month or attend a workshop to enhance your professional skills.

RELATIONSHIPS

- **Lost:** Reflect on shifts in social support or relationship dynamics. Have some relationships ended or changed?

- **Gained:** Recognize new or deepened connections. You may have strengthened bonds with family or made new friends.

- **Create:** Define the type of relationships or community involvement you seek. Consider joining a local club or volunteering, to meet new people and build connections.

SPIRITUAL/RELIGIOUS

- **Lost:** Identify changes in your spiritual practices or faith. Has your approach to spirituality shifted?

- **Gained:** Consider new spiritual insights or practices you have embraced. You might have started meditating or exploring different spiritual texts.

- **Create:** Outline spiritual or religious paths you wish to explore further. Plan regular meditation retreats or join a spiritual study group.

CAREER/HOBBIES

- **Lost:** Note changes in job satisfaction, career direction, or hobbies. Has your career path shifted unexpectedly?

- **Gained:** Acknowledge skills, achievements, or new interests that have emerged. Perhaps you've excelled in a new project or rediscovered an old hobby.

- **Create:** Set objectives for professional goals or hobbies you want to pursue. Consider taking professional development courses or dedicating time each week to a hobby like painting.

FINANCIAL

- **Lost:** Reflect on any financial setbacks experienced. Have you had unexpected expenses or losses?

- **Gained:** Identify any financial improvements or lessons learned. Maybe you've become more budget-conscious or started saving regularly.

- **Create:** Establish goals for financial stability or growth. Outline a plan to increase your savings rate or invest in learning about financial markets.

This practice not only helps in acknowledging and managing the impact of grief but also aids in mapping out a proactive approach to life post-adversity. Each step taken, each reflection noted, builds resilience and prepares you for future challenges, fostering a journey of meaningful transformation and personal growth. Remember, integrating these experiences takes time and patience; proceed at your own pace, allowing your personal growth to unfold naturally.

CHAPTER 10

FINDING THE SUPPORT YOU NEED

SENDING OUT AN SOS

Even in the best of times, it can be hard to ask for help. You may not know what you need, or you might feel that things are so bad that nothing will help. Maybe you don't have the energy, or think you "should" be able to handle this on your own. Sometimes, you don't have anyone you trust enough to confide in, and if you do, you hate being a burden. Getting help is hard, but so is going it alone.

I tend to be stubborn when I need help, especially if it concerns something that I think I "should" have mastered. So, when I rented a kayak and snorkeling gear on the Big Island in Hawaii just a week after my divorce was final, I was confident that I could handle the adventure on my own. There were other kayakers and boats following the same route, so on the off chance I needed help, I could just call out—not that I thought that was even a possibility.

My destination was Ka'awaloa Cove in Kealakekua Bay, known for its pristine reef, tropical fish, and dolphins. It is also home to the Captain Cook memorial. As an experienced kayaker, reaching the cove was no problem. The trouble began when I tried to get out of my kayak to snorkel. As graceful as I tried to be, I flipped the kayak over. Thanks to my meditation practice, I stayed mentally calm and decided to snorkel first and figure out how to right the kayak later. The fish were lovely, and the reef was spectacular.

After I had my fill, I tried to flip my kayak back over by myself. Because I was in the water, and the kayak floating on top, I felt like a small child trying to flip over a sofa. I didn't dare stand on the fragile reef and the shoreline was not a beach, but a cliff. Throughout this, I was silently repeating a mantra. Rationally, I knew I would be fine. I am a good swimmer, I was near the shore, and surrounded by plenty of boats and people. Embarrassed, but knowing I could not flip the boat on my own, I called out a cheery, "Hello! Do you mind helping me?" to a young man snorkeling nearby. He flipped my kayak over like it was a pancake, and went a step further and invited me to use the swim deck of his boat to get back in.

It turned out that my body was not in sync with my mind. I didn't know how badly I was shaking until I was up the stairs and standing on deck. Feeling a little dissociated, I heard someone say, "Give her some water. She is shaking."

I sat down on a bench. After a few sips, I looked up at the kind strangers. As embarrassed as I was—after all I have a kayak at home and even a Coast Guard safety certification, yet here I was needing help—I smiled at them. Connecting with their concerned eyes brought me back. I felt gratitude, and I told them so. Then I looked around at the view, the cliffs, the clear ocean water to ground myself. I got back in my kayak and made the trek back to the cove where I started, and was greeted by the most spectacular sea turtle I ever saw.

I don't need help every time I take a kayak out on the water. Just like you don't need help every time you face a challenge. But sometimes we need to dig deep into our desire to be safe, healthy, or free from suffering, and ask for support. Our minds might tell us that we're okay, that we can power through, but if we drop into our bodies, we often find we are depleted, exhausted, hungry, thirsty, and overwhelmed with emotions. Staying in our minds might allow us to push through temporarily, but it isn't sustainable. We need to pay attention to our whole being: mind, body, and spirit.

THE COST OF NOT HAVING SUPPORT

Many people adapt to life's challenges on their own, and without seeking extra support. And since you have the practices in this book to help you along, you now have skills to help yourself adapt and eventually find a new equilibrium. But whether your loss is the death of someone, the ending of a season, or an ongoing challenge, it is important that you ask yourself the question, "Do I have the support I need?" Drop into your body and ask this, because like my experience in Hawaii, your body may be telling you things your mind is suppressing.

Your body literally feels your emotions, and emotions are the voice of your subconscious. So even if you are not cognitively aware of your fears or unmet needs, your body will try to send you a message. Whether it appears in the form of a sensation, or the lack thereof, ignoring these signals can negatively impact your physical health —causing cardiovascular problems, suppressing your immune system, and leading to so many more somatic ailments—along with your relationships and overall quality of life.

Reaching out for support sooner rather than later can pave the way for a healthier, more resilient tomorrow. Just knowing someone is there to help you flip your metaphorical kayak can bring much needed relief, comfort, and hope. Whether it is a friend, family member, or professional, you need people around you to help navigate the complexities of grief, providing comfort, clarity, and strength. You might be surprised at how quickly you begin to feel better simply because you allowed yourself to receive the help you need.

GETTING GOOD GRIEF SUPPORT

Not all support will be helpful. If someone's attempts to support you are causing you more distress, if their words are judgmental, or if they rely on outdated models of grief, it is likely that their "help" is not actually helpful. You may have experienced this with a friend who insists you should "move on" or "stay strong," ignoring your need to express your emotions. Another friend might constantly change the subject when you try to talk about your loss, making you feel invalidated and unsupported. These reactions can add to your distress rather than alleviate it.

Your friends and family may have the best intentions but won't always know the best way to help. I wasn't the best at providing support myself before I studied thanatology, so now I try to have compassion when I am met with unhelpful advice (and I also use my knowledge to gently educate with compassion). However, when it comes to professionals or peer support groups, set your expectations high.

Unfortunately, not all people who market themselves as "grief experts" actually offer the best support. While many may have good clinical skills, I have heard many stories of "grief therapy gone wrong." Some therapists might adhere strictly to outdated models of grief, such as the idea that grief follows a set of linear stages that you must pass through in a specific order. This approach can make you feel like you're not grieving "correctly" if your experience doesn't match their erroneous criteria. Others might push you to talk about specific details before you are ready. There are also cases where therapists might dismiss your feelings or suggest overly simplistic solutions that don't address the depth of your pain.

Trust your instincts. If someone's attempts at support leave you feeling worse, it's okay to set boundaries and seek out someone who can be more empathetic and understanding. Similarly, if an approach does not resonate with you or is causing additional distress, don't hesitate to look for another source of support that better fits your needs. Advocating for yourself is important, and finding the right support is crucial for your healing journey.

Your comfort and healing are the priority. The guidelines that follow can help you determine if you are receiving the "right" kind of support, knowing that there is no one-size-fits-all approach. They can be used to assess both informal support from friends and family, as well as professional support.

OFFERS DIFFERENT SOLUTIONS FOR DIFFERENT LOSSES

The core principles of support—empathy, validation, and compassionate presence—remain constant for all types of grief support. However, you will have different needs based on whether you are coping with a death, non-death finite loss, or non-death nonfinite loss.

When you are grieving the death of a person or pet, the goal of support is to help you accept the reality of the loss, cope with the pain of grief, adjust to life without this person or animal's physical presence, and establish a continuing bond as you learn how to live again.[16]

Non-death finite loss, such as divorce, job loss, or the end of a significant relationship, requires support that acknowledges the emotional upheaval and assists you in rebuilding a new sense of identity and normalcy. The focus is on validating your loss, assisting you in adapting to changes, encouraging emotional expression, and self-care routines to manage stress and promote well-being.

For non-death nonfinite loss, such as chronic illness, disabilities, infertility, or ongoing trauma, support aims to help you adapt to continuous changes and find ways to live meaningfully despite the persistent nature of your loss. This involves recognizing the ongoing challenges, building resilience, developing adaptive coping strategies, and ensuring long-term support.

Attending loss-specific peer support groups will connect you with people who truly understand your journey. These groups offer a unique environment where shared experiences create a safe space for open, honest conversations. Separate from close family, where feelings might get hurt, peer support groups maintain guidelines and boundaries to ensure everyone feels secure. Additionally, they provide access to specialized tools and resources tailored to your type of loss. Here, you can learn how others are navigating the many changes and ongoing challenges, gaining valuable insights and strategies for your own healing. While personal support systems can sometimes burn out, peer support groups offer sustained, empathetic assistance that fosters resilience and long-term healing.

UNDERSTANDS CONTEMPORARY MODELS OF GRIEF AND LOSS

The more educated someone is about contemporary models and research, the more relevant and helpful the advice will be. Contemporary grief models go beyond the erroneous stages of grief, understanding that grief is non-linear and is different for everyone. This knowledge helps them steer clear of generalizations and platitudes, offering instead insights that are more attuned to your unique experience. They can also dispel common myths about grief.

FACILITATES A HOLISTIC APPROACH

A holistic supporter considers how grief impacts your entire being—mind, body, and spirit. They might encourage you to maintain physical health, which can be neglected during intense emotional turmoil, by suggesting gentle physical activities like walking or yoga. They may provide mental and emotional support by encouraging practices like journaling or meditation, which can help you process feelings. They might also explore the spiritual or existential dimensions of your grief, helping you find meaning or solace in ways that resonate with your beliefs.

COMFORTABLE WITH TOUGH TOPICS

Effective support involves being able to discuss the realities of loss without discomfort. Supporters should not avoid difficult topics or change the subject when you express sadness or anger. They are capable of engaging in conversations about death, the implications of the loss, and the complexities of your feelings. Their willingness to face these topics head-on can make you feel supported and understood in expressing the full range of your grief.

VALUES SPACE AND SILENCE

Silence does not need to be uncomfortable. Good supporters understand the value of simply being present without filling the air with unnecessary words. They allow you to sit with your feelings and process your thoughts in silence, providing a supportive presence that reassures you they are still there for you. This can be comforting when words fail to express the depth of your feelings.

CONSISTENT AND RELIABLE

Consistent and reliable support is crucial, especially during the ups and downs of grief. Whether it's regular check-ins via phone or text, accompanying you to appointments, or just being there at the same time every week for a chat, consistent actions show that supporters are truly committed to your well-being. Reliability in following through on promises also builds trust, making you feel secure in knowing you can depend on them.

RESPECTS YOUR BOUNDARIES

Good support understands and respects your personal space and emotional boundaries. This means that the person supporting you recognizes when to offer help and when to give you room to breathe. They should be sensitive to cues that indicate whether you're open to discussing your feelings or if you need some time alone. It's important for supporters to ask how you're feeling about receiving visitors, discussing your loss, or participating in activities, rather than making assumptions.

Continuously assessing the quality of support you receive helps ensure it meets your evolving needs. What helped you during the initial stages of grief may not be as effective later on. Being open to reassessing and communicating your needs is crucial. This ensures that the support you receive adapts as you change and grow, providing the right kind of help at each stage of your journey.

WHEN TO REACH OUT FOR PROFESSIONAL SUPPORT

Just as the young man helped me flip my kayak and get back to shore, your friends and family can offer comfort, perspective, and practical assistance. However, even if you have a supportive personal network, working with a skilled and compassionate professional can provide additional, invaluable benefits. Professionals bring expertise and specialized tools to help you navigate your emotions and challenges more effectively. They ensure you receive comprehensive support tailored to your unique needs. In a safe space, professionals guide you through your emotions, offer expert advice, and equip you with effective coping strategies. Their support can be transformative in navigating the complexities of grief, helping you find clarity, resilience, and healing.

Persistent sadness or depression is a significant indicator that you may need to seek help from a professional. While it is normal to feel sad after a loss, if your mood remains low or continues to decline over an extended period, it might be a sign that you could benefit from professional support. In some cases, grief can lead to a prolonged state of depression if not addressed. Seeking support from friends, family, or professionals can provide relief and new coping strategies.

Another reason to seek support is consistently feeling overwhelmed by everyday tasks. If simple activities or decisions that you used to handle with ease now feel insurmountable, it indicates that the emotional weight of your grief is affecting your daily functioning—and signals that you might benefit from additional support.

One way to check if your mood is grief- or depression-related is to ask yourself: "Would all my problems be solved if this loss situation were reversed and everything went back to normal?" However, if you had any type of diagnosis before the loss or feel your distress is getting worse, please consult a professional for an assessment. This is especially crucial if you are thinking of harming yourself or someone else, experiencing intrusive thoughts, or having visual or auditory hallucinations. In these cases, seek out a mental health professional who can screen you for Post-Traumatic Stress Disorder (PTSD) or other conditions that extend beyond grief itself.

As discussed in Chapter 4, somatic symptoms are common with emotional distress. Fatigue, changes in appetite, or sleep disturbances can be normal physical manifestations of your grief. If you feel your physical health is at risk or declining, please see your healthcare provider. Addressing these symptoms with a professional can improve how you feel, giving you more resources to manage the physical and emotional aspects of grief more effectively.

WHERE TO FIND PROFESSIONAL HELP

The importance of finding a skilled practitioner cannot be overstated. Grief is a complex and deeply personal experience. A skilled practitioner understands the importance of building a trusting relationship, can tailor their approach to suit individual needs, and provides a safe space for mourners to explore their deepest emotions without judgment. This level of understanding and accommodation helps individuals feel supported and understood, which is crucial for healing. Taking the time to find the right professional—someone who's not only professionally qualified but also a good fit personally—or a peer support group that you feel comfortable with can be an important step in addressing the multifaceted nature of grief and moving toward recovery.

Professional support can come from a variety of sources, each with their specific expertise in dealing with the nuances of grief. Professionals certified by the Association of Death Education and Counseling as either Certified in Thanatology (CT) or Fellow in Thanatology (FT) credential can be highly beneficial. People like myself hold a Master's Degree in thanatology and may be certified in another modality that has a counseling model.

Psychologists and counselors, especially those trained in bereavement therapy, offer personalized strategies to manage grief based on therapeutic models and their extensive understanding of emotional health. Grief therapists might use approaches such as cognitive-behavioral therapy (CBT) or acceptance and commitment therapy (ACT) to help individuals process their emotions in constructive ways.

In addition to traditional therapists, there are grief coaches and specialized grief counselors who focus solely on helping people navigate their bereavement. These professionals can provide specific guidance and practical advice around grief, helping individuals set realistic goals for their emotional recovery and providing tools to handle daily challenges. For those who prefer group settings, joining a support group facilitated by a skilled therapist or counselor can offer the comfort of shared experiences, making it easier to discuss feelings and coping strategies in a safe, empathetic environment.

If your loss is due to a death, hospices play a vital role in community bereavement support, offering services not only to families of the deceased who were in their care, but also to anyone in the community who is grieving. Many hospice programs provide both group and individual sessions as part of their bereavement support, making them a valuable resource for those in need of compassionate guidance.

PRACTICE:
CRAFTING YOUR STORY TO SHARE

Sharing your grief story is a powerful tool for healing and connecting with others. By focusing on the most important details ahead of time, you can ensure that your story effectively communicates your needs and emotions, whether you're grieving a death, adjusting to a non-death loss, or coping with a nonfinite, ongoing challenge. Writing your story in a journal before meeting up with a friend or therapist can help you organize your thoughts and feel more confident in sharing.

This practice isn't the place to hold back. It's about getting everything out so you can then decide what you want to share. Don't overthink it—write what comes naturally without editing it first. You can always make a list of what you want to share and leave out what you don't. Use the questions below to guide your journaling process.

SET THE SCENE

1. Start by setting the context for your grief. Describe who or what you lost, such as a loved one, a job, a relationship, or your identity. Include when this loss occurred or began. For ongoing challenges like caregiving or chronic illness, describe your day-to-day challenges as well as what you have to relinquish to cope with the ongoing changes. This helps the listener understand the background and significance of your experience.

DESCRIBE YOUR REACTION

2. Next, describe your initial reactions to the loss. Reflect on how you felt in the moments and days following the event, whether it was the death of a loved one or the end of a significant chapter in your life. If you're dealing with the onset of an ongoing stressor, explain your initial feelings and reactions to this continuous challenge. Be honest about your emotions, as this helps convey the depth of your grief.

EXPLAIN YOUR CURRENT STATE

3. Since your initial reaction, reflect on where you started and where you are now. Describe how your feelings have evolved over time. Highlight any challenges, obstacles, or surprising developments you've encountered along the way. This deeper reflection will help you share how you are currently feeling.

IDENTIFY WHAT TYPE OF SUPPORT YOU NEED

4. Reflect on what would help you the most at this moment. Think about your current feelings and challenges. Do you need someone to listen without judgment, provide understanding, offer specific advice, or give practical help? Consider what would make you feel more understood and cared for. Clearly identifying your needs can guide the conversation and set expectations.

REVIEW YOUR STORY

5. Read through your story and make notes. Reflect on how it reads and if it clearly conveys your emotions and needs. This will help you refine your narrative and ensure it captures the essence of your experience.

CHOOSE WHAT TO SHARE

6. Decide which parts of your story you want to share. Consider your audience and the context in which you'll be sharing. Focus on the key emotions and needs that are most relevant to your current situation. This will help you communicate your experience more effectively and set clear expectations for the support you seek.

Expressing your grief helps you connect with others and garner the support you need. Your story is a powerful tool for fostering understanding and empathy, paving the way for deeper connections and mutual healing. Sharing your story is not only a step toward healing for you but also a way to deepen connections with those around you, allowing them to walk alongside you in your journey of grief.

CHAPTER 11

HOW TO HELP OTHERS NAVIGATE LOSS

THE COURAGE TO BE WITH PAIN

Just as loss is an unavoidable part of your own life, there will inevitably come a time when someone you deeply care for is in need of a friend to accompany them through their grief. This call to service can feel daunting, even when you have a strong desire to help. Even among the best of friends, there can be hesitation, rooted in a sense of "I don't know how to help" or "I am afraid to say the wrong thing." What I hope to impart is that companioning others is not about being helpful or saying the right thing, but about aligning your efforts with their needs.

When we are called to help someone in need, we don't need to try to fix the unfixable. Instead, we can simply look inside ourselves for the blend of strength and vulnerability that I call skillful courage. This involves the strength to acknowledge your fears, and the vulnerability to tap into the part of you that cares enough to stay present in the face of great suffering. It is also an invitation for you to tap into the part of your heart that is intimately familiar with the pain of loss. The purpose of connecting with your own grief is not to center yourself or offer unsolicited advice; it's so you can provide the same comforting presence you needed during your darkest times.

If you are too raw with your own grief, it is important that you recognize your limits. There may be seasons in your life when you are not capable of providing support to another. Trying to support others when you are emotionally depleted may not be beneficial for either party involved. In such instances, most often the best course of action is to communicate your limitations compassionately, while assuring the other person that you care deeply. While this does not guarantee a perfect outcome, it does reduce the chances for a misunderstanding rooted in a perception that you do not care.

AVOID UNSOLICITED ADVICE

It is rarely helpful to tell anyone what they should feel or do, the exception being when their safety is at stake. No matter how well-intentioned, unsolicited advice often feels overwhelming or even dismissive to the person on the receiving end.

So much of the advice that circulates is shaped by popular culture, often informed by outdated or oversimplified understandings of a deeply personal and complex process. One of the most well-known examples of this is the continued proliferation of the "Five Stages of Grief" introduced by Elisabeth Kübler-Ross—denial, anger, bargaining, depression, and acceptance. While Dr Kübler-Ross deserves the utmost respect for the work she did to advocate for dying patients during a time when they were marginalized and misunderstood, she herself noted that these stages were not meant to rigidly define the grieving "process" (grief is not a process; it's an experience). They do not necessarily occur in order, nor does every individual experience all of them. Additionally, her observations were of dying patients, not grieving people.

Some people may find this framework helpful, and I do not want to diminish a construct that brings someone comfort as they navigate their grief. However, I think it is important to acknowledge that the modern study of death, dying, and bereavement, known as thanatology, prefers more spacious models that are focused on tasks, learning, and meaning reconstruction (see page 82); it avoids prescribing what one should feel.

Unless you are asked otherwise, simply offer your presence. Let the other person lead the conversation. Just showing up, ready to listen and comfort without judgment is one of the most powerful forms of support. Of course, few will find it offensive if you show up with their favorite creature comfort, be it chocolate, their preferred type of tea, or a cozy blanket, to remind them that someone else cares for them when they are alone.

A GENTLE GLANCE INWARD

The journey to help someone else through grief begins with cultivating compassion—and we cannot extend to others what we do not offer to ourselves. As you learned in Chapter 6, self-compassion teaches us to recognize our own suffering without judgment or criticism. With mindfulness, common humanity, and self-kindness (see page 69), we can remember that feeling overwhelmed or uncertain in the face of loss does not mean we are broken; it means we are human.

If you are critical of your own feelings of loss or doubt your ability to be present for someone else, you inadvertently erect barriers around your heart. If you struggle to connect deeply with your own emotions, you are more likely to retreat than reach out. On the other hand, when you accept your own emotions and limitations with kindness and understanding, you are better equipped to be present and supportive. By embracing your own vulnerabilities, you open yourself up to truly understand and share in the pain of others. This openness is the foundation of genuine support.

STEER CLEAR OF PLATITUDES

Often, well-intentioned attempts to provide comfort through common sayings are more often dismissive and shaming rather than kind. Phrases such as "Everything happens for a reason," or "This will make you stronger," or "They are in a better place now" are charged with toxic positivity. Platitudes de-legitimize pain and promote emotional avoidance by verbally pushing the person's very real feelings away.

Many platitudes are not only dismissive, but they are also inaccurate. For example, "time heals all wounds" is simply untrue. Modern grief theory tells us that it is not merely the passage of time, but what one does with that time that matters. Research by Dr Robert Neimeyer suggests that time contributes only minimally, about 1%, to someone learning to adapt to their loss, whereas actively engaging with your grief through reflection, seeking support, or personal growth activities is far more beneficial than passively waiting for time to heal the pain. Instead of using scripted expressions, presence is most effective. You can demonstrate genuine compassion by showing up, being emotionally available, and listening without trying to change how the person feels.

BE SPECIFIC WITH OFFERS OF HELP

In the immediate aftermath of a loss, your deepest wish might be to undo what has happened. Beyond that, it can be profoundly difficult to pinpoint what you need. The intense emotions and overwhelming nature of grief can obscure your ability to think clearly and recognize the type of support that would be most beneficial. Often, you may not even know what would help, or you may hesitate to request assistance for fear of imposing on others.

These challenges are also common among those experiencing nonfinite loss, where the sense of loss is ongoing and chronic. During these vulnerable times, the ubiquitous offer of "Let me know if you need anything" may sound well-intentioned, but shifts the onus to the person who needs help, adding stress during an already challenging period.

Instead of making an open-ended offer, it's more helpful to propose specific actions like, "I'm bringing dinner over tomorrow night. What kind of cheese would you like on your burger?" or "I'm planning to go to the grocery store for you on Wednesday. Let's chat beforehand so I can pick up exactly what you need." This approach provides concrete assistance and significantly eases the daily burdens. Where non-specific offers can leave people feeling frustrated that they cannot articulate or even understand what they need, providing specific, actionable support is a more effective approach.

AVOID COMPARING LOSSES

Comparison may be a natural human instinct, but it is rarely helpful in the space of grief. On the contrary, when it comes to supporting someone in their sorrow, comparison can be detrimental. This is because it can undermine the unique and personal nature of an individual's grief, potentially depriving them of the genuine empathy and understanding they need. Additionally, it can result in an inadvertent role-reversal, where the person you were trying to comfort is put in the untimely position of comforting you.

When you share your own grief story, staying grounded is vital (see page 124). It allows you to remain connected to the current situation and ensures that your sharing doesn't overshadow the person's unique experience or turn the focus away from their needs to your own.

It is important to recognize that while some people may not want to hear about your own grief as they are processing their own, others may find it helps them feel more connected. Like giving advice, it is crucial to get consent before sharing your personal experiences.

SUPPORTING THROUGH THE LONG TERM

Understanding that grief does not adhere to a predictable timeline and that the needs of the grieving person can evolve dramatically over time is crucial for providing meaningful support. Whether the loss involves the death of a loved one or significant non-death losses, such as divorce, job loss, or a major life transition, most people will appreciate support that goes beyond the first few days, weeks, or months.

It is normal for support needs to change over time. In the case of death-related losses, immediate support might involve being physically present, handling daily chores, or simply listening. As time moves on, support needs to adapt to include remembering that significant dates can stir up grief even if the event is long past. These anniversary reactions often begin well before the date itself, and usually include feelings of restlessness and anxiety. Regular check-ins, such as sending a message just to share a memory or calling on important dates, can also be deeply meaningful. This kind of ongoing engagement reassures the grieving person that they are not alone and that their loss is still acknowledged, helping them feel supported as they continue to navigate their grief.

For non-death losses, such as the end of a marriage or significant career changes, support might initially focus on practical help, like assisting with moving homes or updating résumés. Over the longer term, helping to recognize and commemorate milestones in their new life can be equally important. For instance, commemorating the finalization of a divorce if appropriate, or the first day in a new job can help acknowledge the transition and reinforce support. Continued encouragement as they establish new routines and rebuild their identity post-loss shows an understanding that the loss profoundly affects their life.

In both types of losses, long-term support means maintaining patience and understanding, providing a consistent presence that adapts to the changing dynamics of grief. It's about ensuring that the individual feels no pressure to conform to societal expectations of "moving on" but instead feels supported throughout their unique journey of grief and recovery. Not only does this approach help them heal at their own pace, but it also affirms that they do not have to face their challenges alone.

PRACTICE:
SUPPORTING A GRIEVING PERSON

Your presence is the greatest asset you can offer someone going through a difficult time. Showing up provides them with a sense of connection and support during a time when many others will turn away. Being present means creating a space where individual, cultural, and other differences are honored and respected. You may know how helpful this is from your own loss.

And yet, it can be hard to know what to do or say when nothing can be fixed. It is also hard to see someone you care about hurting. And since most of us were not taught how to accompany our own emotions, much less others, you may not know just how to show up effectively and sustainably. Like learning how to navigate your own grief, companioning others is a skill you can learn.

The tips that follow will help you stay present and supportive. However, this practice is not about memorizing the list of tips below, which will give you guidance, but embodying a mindful presence when you visit someone going through an unexpected and unwelcome change. The most important thing beyond showing up is to stay kind, open, and curious, honoring the unique needs and preferences of the person you are supporting.

BEFORE YOU BEGIN

Remember your intention: Before engaging in conversation, remind yourself of your intention to support and listen. This isn't about fixing their pain or offering solutions; it's about being there for them. Keeping this intention clear can help guide your interactions and keep you focused on their needs rather than your reactions.

Acknowledge your filters: Recognize that your own experiences with grief may color your interactions. This is not to assign a value of right or wrong, good or bad, but to highlight that we all have filters that influence how we respond to someone else's grief. Be mindful of this and strive to keep your focus on the person you are supporting, ensuring that their needs take precedence. This awareness helps prevent your own biases from overshadowing the support you aim to provide.

Embrace a non-fixing attitude: It's important to remember that you are not there to fix the situation. Grief is a natural response to loss, not a problem to be solved. By accepting that there is nothing inherently wrong that needs correcting, you can allow the person grieving to express their feelings without the pressure of needing to be "cured" or rushed through their process.

WHILE COMPANIONING

Engage in active listening: Active listening involves paying full attention to the speaker, understanding their message, responding thoughtfully, and remembering what was said. This practice helps in truly witnessing the depth of their experience and showing that you value their feelings and words.

Offer space for silence: Don't be afraid of silence. Grieving individuals may need pauses to gather their thoughts or compose themselves. Silence can be a powerful tool that allows the person to feel safe and understood without the pressure to keep talking.

Be mindful of your responses: When you do respond, slow down and choose your words carefully to ensure they are supportive and empathetic. Avoid the urge to relate everything back to your own experiences. Before you share something personal, ask yourself whether you are sharing it because of your need, or because you truly believe it would be helpful for the grieving person to hear. Instead, focus on what the grieving person is sharing with you. By being mindful and deliberate in your responses, you can offer more meaningful and compassionate support.

Reflect back what you hear: Occasionally, it can be helpful to reflect back what you've heard to show that you are listening and to clarify your understanding. This can be as simple as, "It sounds like you're feeling really lost without them," which can validate their feelings and promote further expression. Even repeating one key word and then leaving space can be helpful, such as saying "lost … " and allowing them to continue sharing their thoughts and feelings.

Maintain embodied awareness: Throughout the conversation, maintain awareness of your own body. Feel your feet on the floor, notice your breath, and consciously relax your muscles when you notice tension. This physical awareness can prevent you from becoming overwhelmed and help you stay tuned in to the conversation. Compassion requires knowing that you are separate from the person you are supporting—not to "other" them—but to give you enough distance to be supportive without falling into empathetic overwhelm. This balance allows you to offer genuine, sustainable support while protecting your own emotional well-being.

Tend to your own discomfort: Listening to intense emotions can be uncomfortable. Recognize any discomfort that arises in you and use your senses to become present. Feel your breath and your body. Look at an object in the room for five seconds and notice its details. Listen to the sounds around you. You can also use a mantra, such as "Right now I am present with my friend," to help ground yourself. These mindfulness techniques can help you stay calm and present, enabling you to provide better support in the moment. Remember to tend to your own emotions later, giving yourself the care and space you need

Stay connected to your purpose: Keep connecting back to why you are there. You are there to provide support and companionship during a difficult time, not to judge, analyze, or interpret their grief. This purposeful presence can make all the difference to someone who is feeling isolated in their pain.

CHAPTER 12

THE GLOBAL LANDSCAPE OF LOSS

COLLECTIVE GRIEF

The sorrow of tragedy has no borders. From natural disasters and political unrest to climate change and religious oppression, unwelcome changes from all around the world merge collective sorrow with personal grief. Mass shootings, genocide, outbreaks, wars, and pervasive social injustices—such as racism, sexism, ageism, ableism, classism, and heterosexism—shake the very foundations of our safety and identity. This widespread upheaval challenges our sense of belonging and stability, deepening our experience of loss on both a personal and global scale.

Even if you are trying to focus on navigating your personal losses, it is hard to escape the relentless cycle of breaking news and commentary on social media, where the stream of updates is constant and often overwhelming. Each notification, each "breaking" headline begs for our attention, and the information is delivered so fast we have no time to recover emotionally before the next piece of bad news hits.

Consciously or not, we make a choice. Either we pause to acknowledge the impact of each piece of bad news, we keep scrolling as one headline swiftly replaces the next, while we tune out and try to not feel anything at all, or we put our phone down and turn away. There can be a sense of unity when we collectively mourn, both online and in public. But if you are already coping with a personal loss, this added weight of collective grief can intensify your own grief, making it harder to find space for personal healing. As you learned earlier in this book, it is important to address any loss that you deem important. Whether it is a celebrity that wrote the soundtrack to your teenage years, a world leader you respected, or a whole region of human beings marginalized by oppressors, if it matters to you it is worth tending to.

ASHLEY'S STORY:
PERSONAL AND COLLECTIVE LOSS

In late 2016, my client Ashley was in an online relationship with Jeremy, a man she never met in person, but who lived just half an hour away. About six months into their text-based and telephone romance, he suddenly stopped calling. Naturally, Ashley was in distress, and assumed he had ghosted her. A few days later, however, she received a text from a woman who identified herself as Jeremy's sister. She had found their exchanges on his phone and wanted to let Ashley know that Jeremy had died from a heart condition. Ashley was devastated and bewildered. Her grief experience was understandably complex, and her pain disenfranchised by the few people she dared to tell.

Our weekly visits were a safe space for Ashley to discuss her grief, confusion, and the many questions that arose as she learned more about Jeremy posthumously through his family and friends that she met at the funeral. Her grief was raw and acute, but a few days after the 2016 US presidential election, her demeanor changed. When she walked into the studio she said, "I don't need to talk about Jeremy today, I feel like I am going to have a panic attack over the election." This was the first time she—or any of my clients dealing with fresh grief—shifted focus from personal loss to something national. It was not the last. While self-compassion is a vital practice for navigating personal grief, compassion serves a similar purpose for collective loss, giving us a skillful way to respond to situations we cannot change.

Ashley's shift from personal grief to the collective anxiety triggered by the election illustrates how deeply interconnected our personal experiences are with larger societal events. This blending of personal and collective suffering is not just theoretical, but a very real challenge that many of us face. It brings to light the need for resilience strategies not just for individual losses but also for the shared traumas that touch us all.

Ashley and I explored how the practices she was using to cope with her individual grief—mindfulness, self-compassion, and somatic yoga—could also help ease her anxiety about global events. She limited her news consumption to just five minutes a day, rather than watching television for hours. The most transformative practice for her was incorporating metta, the compassion and loving-kindness meditation (see page 132), into her routine. Through these strategies, Ashley found a balance, allowing herself to process both her personal and collective grief.

TENDING TO COLLECTIVE SUFFERING WITH COMPASSION

The constant exposure to the suffering of others can lead to compassion fatigue, the emotional and physical depletion that comes from constant caring and empathy without sufficient personal replenishment. I experienced this firsthand when I volunteered for the New Orleans Suicide Hotline just after Hurricane Katrina. At the time, I was already working as a suicide call specialist for the Frederick County Mental Health Association. Most of the calls I received were from people in desperate need of food or financial assistance. We volunteers were informed that the organizations we typically referred callers to were temporarily out of funds. Relaying this message, while also providing these organizations' contact information for future reference, was incredibly challenging. The inability to offer the immediate help these callers needed plunged me into a deep, dark place.

This was before I knew anything about compassion fatigue, and the overwhelming feeling of ineffectiveness quickly began to wear me down. To numb these feelings, I turned to alcohol: beer the first night, wine the second, and liquor by the third. When I returned home, I was deeply disconnected from myself—my eyes were heavy, and I felt detached from my body, as though observing myself from a distance. I reached out to my supervisor, who compassionately helped me recognize that I was experiencing compassion fatigue. I decided to take a break from the hotline and worked with my therapist to address the trauma.

As I acknowledged in the prologue of this book, it's important to recognize that this is not the most tragic of tales. I was safe, well-fed, alive, and had a home to return to—a stark contrast to the dire circumstances faced by many New Orleans residents, as well as numerous first responders and volunteers. For a time, I carried the shame of numbing my pain with alcohol, but I've come to understand that, in the moment, it seemed like the only way I knew how to cope. I can now offer compassion to that earlier version of myself, understanding the context and pressures I faced.

I actually have some gratitude for what I learned. Not only do I have tools to help myself when faced with collective pain, but I also love sharing this knowledge with my clients and other professionals through workshops and keynotes on coping with personal, professional, and collective losses—because now I know what I would do differently.

WHAT WE CAN DO

Just as Ashley needed to find ways to cope with both her personal grief and the communal distress, and I needed to recognize the effect of compassion fatigue, we all need to manage the weight of collective suffering.

PRACTICE COMPASSION

Sometimes, it feels good to do something tangible, like sending money, volunteering to help, or writing a letter to your political representative. But as my story illustrates, this doesn't always get to the root of the suffering. Compassion is not about doing; it is about embodying—really feeling—an intention to reduce suffering, even if you cannot change anything. Compassion isn't about fixing things because sometimes we simply can't.

There are three steps to cultivating compassion. The first step begins with **noticing suffering**. This initial stage involves becoming aware of another's pain, recognizing that someone is experiencing distress. It's about tuning in and acknowledging the presence of suffering without immediately seeking solutions. This awareness is a crucial first step, as it allows us to connect with the reality of the situation.

The second step is **feeling**. This means allowing ourselves to empathize with the person in distress, to feel their pain and share in their emotional experience. This emotional connection can be deeply moving and sometimes overwhelming, but it is essential to fully engage with the suffering.

The third step is **responding**. This does not always mean fixing the problem. Responding compassionately might involve offering emotional support, such as listening and validating the person's feelings, taking practical action, or simply feeling a heartfelt desire for their suffering to end. In the Buddhist practice of metta (see page 132), you send out well wishes. Responding means expressing care and a willingness to help, even when the situation cannot be immediately resolved.

Humans are biologically wired for compassion because it benefits our survival. If no one was willing to help another person out, our species would cease to exist. When we engage in compassionate actions, our bodies release oxytocin, sometimes called the "love hormone." This hormone promotes feelings of bonding and reduces stress. Compassion also activates brain regions associated with reward and pleasure, reinforcing positive social interactions and strengthening our connections with others. By cultivating compassion, we not only help those around us but also enhance our own well-being, fostering a sense of belonging and resilience.

BE PRESENT TO OUR LIVES AND LOVED ONES

In the midst of global grief, it is essential to stay engaged with our immediate surroundings and cherish the connections we have with our loved ones. This engagement acts as a vital counterbalance to the often overwhelming nature of worldwide suffering. By focusing on the present moment and fostering strong relationships with those around us, we can create a sanctuary of stability and love that not only supports our own mental health but also strengthens our resilience. This presence ensures that despite the global scale of grief, we do not lose sight of the beauty and joy that personal relationships can offer.

SELF-CARE: SUSTAINING EMPATHY AND ACTION

Maintaining our physical and emotional well-being is not just an act of self-preservation but a necessity to sustain our capacity for empathy and action. Self-care practices such as regular physical activity, adequate sleep, balanced nutrition, and mindfulness exercises are crucial. These habits help us recharge and clear our minds, making us more effective in our empathetic engagements and activities. When we are well-cared-for, our ability to support others and to contribute meaningfully to alleviating global suffering is enhanced significantly.

Finally, encouraging active engagement in causes that address the roots of global suffering underscores the importance of not only understanding but also acting on the issues at hand. Activism can take many forms, from local community efforts to international advocacy, and each action contributes to a larger solution. By participating in or supporting movements that aim to alleviate suffering—be it through advocacy, volunteering, or educating others—we not only find a constructive outlet for our grief but also contribute to meaningful change. This active involvement is empowering, as it helps us regain a sense of control and purpose in the face of global challenges.

HOLDING ON TO HOPE

Together, we navigate the dual realities of personal and global grief. By staying present in our lives, prioritizing self-care, practicing compassion, and engaging in activism, we can manage the impact of global tragedies while fostering an environment ripe for healing and positive change. I believe in the potential for growth and healing within each of us, and by cultivating these practices, we not only enhance our own well-being but also contribute to the healing of our world. Each step we take strengthens us individually and collectively, equipping us to face challenges with resilience and hope.

Finding a balance between engaging with the world's suffering and nurturing our own well-being is essential. This balance ensures that while we actively participate in addressing global issues, we do not lose ourselves in the process. Our individual health and happiness are deeply intertwined with the state of the world, making self-care a crucial part of creating a healthier, more compassionate planet.

Let us hold on to hope and remain resilient, knowing that every act of kindness, no matter how small, contributes to the collective healing of our planet. In a world often beset by seemingly insurmountable challenges, these acts of kindness and courage are the threads that weave together a tapestry of recovery and peace. Remember, each step forward in caring for ourselves and each other propels us along the path to a healed and harmonious world. Keep moving forward, keep caring, and continue to add your unique voice to the chorus calling for change. Together, we can make a difference.

And let's not forget to extend compassion to ourselves. You are an inhabitant of this Earth. You matter. As we traverse this terrain—much like navigating a challenging but beautiful hiking trail—it's vital to pause occasionally, to look around, and to take care of not just our surroundings but also ourselves. Just as we wear sturdy boots to protect our steps along rocky paths, we must also armor ourselves with kindness and care to sustain our journey.

PRACTICE:
METTA MEDITATION

Metta meditation, or loving-kindness meditation, is a cherished practice rooted in the Buddhist tradition, designed to cultivate unconditional love and kindness toward all beings. As you engage in this practice, you'll find it a powerful tool for enhancing empathy, reducing negative emotions, and fostering a sense of interconnectedness. This form of meditation is especially beneficial during personal and global crises, as it encourages a deep, compassionate response to suffering—both your own and that of others.

In metta meditation, you start by directing feelings of goodwill and kindness toward yourself and gradually extend these feelings to others—friends, family, strangers, and even those with whom you might have difficulties. The practice unfolds in six key directions, enhancing your emotional resilience and broadening your compassion. By focusing on positive, loving energy, you help dissolve the barriers of anger, resentment, and isolation that are often heightened by global tragedies.

As you practice metta, remember that each phrase you silently repeat—wishing happiness, health, safety, and ease—is a step toward greater peace, both within your heart and in the external world. This not only boosts your own well-being but also contributes to a more loving and peaceful world. Engage with this practice regularly and observe how it transforms your approach to challenges, enhancing your capacity to care for yourself and others in a profound and meaningful way.

BEGIN WITH A BENEVOLENT BEING

1. Before focusing on yourself, it can be helpful to start by visualizing a benevolent being—this could be a spiritual figure, a revered teacher, or any being that embodies pure compassion and wisdom. Direct loving-kindness toward them with phrases like:

"May you be happy, as I wish to be happy.
May you be healthy, as I wish to be healthy.
May you be safe, as I wish to be safe.
May you live with ease, as I wish to live with ease."

This initial step warms up your heart and prepares you for deeper practice.

TURN LOVING-KINDNESS TOWARD YOURSELF

2. Sit in a comfortable and quiet space. Close your eyes and take a few deep breaths to center yourself. Begin to direct feelings of kindness and love toward yourself. Silently repeat:

"May I be happy, as I wish to be happy.
May I be healthy, as I wish to be healthy.
May I be safe, as I wish to be safe.
May I live with ease, as I wish to live with ease."

Feel the sincerity of the words and nurture your own happiness and well-being.

EXTEND TO A FRIEND OR FAMILY MEMBER

3. Next, bring to mind someone you love—a friend or a family member. Direct the same loving-kindness phrases toward them:

"May you be happy, as I wish to be happy.
May you be healthy, as I wish to be healthy.
May you be safe, as I wish to be safe.
May you live with ease, as I wish to live with ease."

Visualize your loving-kindness as a gentle light spreading from your heart to theirs, nurturing and supporting them.

INCLUDE A NEUTRAL PERSON

4. Now, think of someone neutral in your life, someone you neither like nor dislike, perhaps someone you see regularly but don't know well. Extend the same phrases of loving-kindness to them, acknowledging their basic humanity and your shared desire for happiness and safety.

OFFER LOVING-KINDNESS TO A DIFFICULT PERSON

5. Carefully choose someone you have mild difficulties with—not your worst enemy. This practice is about breaking down barriers of resentment and opening your heart, but it should not be overwhelming. Again, extend:

"May you be happy, as I wish to be happy.
May you be healthy, as I wish to be healthy.
May you be safe, as I wish to be safe.
May you live with ease, as I wish to live with ease."

This step is challenging but cultivates deep compassion and understanding.

EMBRACE ALL BEINGS

6. Finally, expand your loving-kindness to encompass all beings around the world. Envision your compassionate feelings radiating outward, enveloping the entire Earth.

"May all beings be happy, as I wish to be happy.
May all beings be healthy, as I wish to be healthy.
May all beings be safe, as I wish to be safe.
May all beings live with ease, as I wish to live with ease."

This universal goodwill is the essence of metta, fostering a profound connection to all life.

EPILOGUE

THE PATH
AHEAD

MOVING FORWARD

The 2024 solar eclipse left portions of the United States awestruck, including my town of Falling Waters, West Virginia. Many people stopped to witness this rare phenomenon, whether drawn to it from a scientific or spiritual place of interest.

The symbolic meaning of a solar eclipse varies depending on who you ask and the time period in which the belief originated. The Ancient Greeks believed that an eclipse was a sign that the gods were displeased, and misfortune would follow. Similarly, Navajo elders instruct their community to stay indoors during an eclipse, seeing it as a sacred interaction between the sun and the moon. They use this time for quiet reflection and to share traditional stories, rooted in their profound respect for the cosmic order. In Hindu mythology, eclipses are thought to occur when the demon Rahu devours the sun, symbolizing a temporary triumph of darkness over light. In East Asia, eclipses are regarded as a time of renewal and a sign of positive change, believed to wash away past troubles and herald new beginnings. This perspective deeply resonates with me.

Like many people, I have always been enamored with the stars. During my undergraduate studies at St Mary's College of Maryland, I enrolled in two astronomy courses with the inspirational Dr Humm that focused on the mathematical equations and principles of physics that rule the sky. While I marvel at the mathematical elegance with which the universe operates, the vast mysteries it holds captivate me even more.

Although the moon, sun, and earth were not perfectly aligned in my region, and the sky never went fully dark, the crescent shape of our closest star was nothing short of spectacular. In order to both record and view the event safely, I toggled the pro settings on my phone's camera and placed it on a tripod in my front yard, which overlooks the Potomac River. Partial cloud cover frequently obscured the union, but in the space between the clouds was a sacred sight indeed.

As the moon began to cross in front of the sun, partially obscuring its light, I felt a surge of inspiration. I lifted my arms out to the side and, in a moment of spontaneity, began what I can only describe as an incantation:

"The time before this was before times. The time from this moment on is after those times. And things are going to be different now, because I am different now. I am taking back my power."

Or something like that. The exact words have faded from my memory, and while I know it was likely captured on the phone's video, I haven't dared to replay it. Call me superstitious, but I feel that revisiting that moment will diminish its power. Plus, it isn't the actual words I spoke that mattered, but my intention and how I felt as I shed the old energy and embraced the new. And indeed, things have been different in the few months since. I have actively embraced the intention I released into the sky.

This simple, spontaneous act under the eclipsed sky marked a turning point, a commitment to change, renewal, and growth. Specifically, I am working on relinquishing my codependent behaviors, worrying less about what people might think, and learning how to meet my own needs. Focusing on myself has been both a challenging and rewarding journey. In this space of self-reflection and growth, I am nurturing the parts of me that were once neglected. Healing the trauma from my past has been like piecing together a mosaic—each fragment, no matter how broken, contributes to the whole picture of who I am today.

It has been two years since my divorce and five since my estrangement with my father. These milestones mark a period of profound change and healing in my life. Living by the river now, I find solace in the gentle flow of the water, a constant reminder of life's continuity and the beauty of finding peace within oneself. The river, which looks different every day, mirrors my journey. Just as it carves its path through the landscape, I am carving a new path for myself, one that honors my past but is not defined by it. The serenity of my surroundings helps me to practice mindfulness, to stay grounded in the present, and to appreciate the small moments of joy and contentment that now fill my days.

I have learned the importance of self-compassion, of treating myself with the same kindness and understanding that I would offer a dear friend. This practice has been a cornerstone of my healing, allowing me to forgive myself for the perceived failures and to celebrate my resilience and strength.

Each day, I make a conscious effort to reconnect with my inner self, to listen to my needs and to honor them. Whether through journaling, meditation, or swimming in the water, I find ways to nurture my spirit and to heal the wounds of the past. This journey of self-discovery has shown me that true happiness and fulfillment come from within, and that I am capable of creating a life that is rich in meaning and joy.

I cannot end this book with a story about finding my one true love, or reveal that my father and I have reconciled. But I can with certainty say that I am happy. Happier than I have ever been, in fact, with myself. I am open to love when it comes again, but it no longer defines who I am as it once did. Nor do I need approval from my father, because now I get that from within.

Throughout these pages, we have explored the unseen terrains of loss—those that society often overlooks, yet leave indelible marks on your soul. From the shattering pain of a loved one's death to the subtle, but equally profound, losses of dreams, relationships, and identities, each step has been a testament to your strength and willingness to embrace what is. I want to acknowledge the courage it takes for you to walk this path. This is the kind of courage that comes without choice. Grief, in all its forms, reshapes you in ways you could never have imagined. Yet, it is through these profound transformations that you discover the depths of your resilience and the boundless capacity of your heart to heal and love again. While you don't choose your losses, putting this knowledge into practice is a choice—and a powerful one at that.

I invite you to reflect on the practices you now have at your disposal: the grounding power of mindfulness, the expressive freedom of journaling, the soothing balm of creative rituals, and the sustaining grace of self-compassion. These tools are not merely exercises but pathways to reconnect with the essence of who you are, beyond the pain and sorrow. While nothing can guarantee that your life will be free from loss and pain, my hope is that you now have an idea of how to tend to your suffering.

Grief becomes a part of the landscape of our lives. But in learning to navigate this terrain with care and intention, you create a new path—one where grief and joy coexist, where endings lead to beginnings, and where love continues to shine through the darkest forests of our broken hearts. There will be days when the weight of loss feels unbearable, and there will be moments of unexpected lightness and joy. Allow yourself the grace to experience both. Trust that each step, no matter how small, is a vital part of your journey.

May you find peace in the presence of your loved ones, comfort in the rituals that connect you to your past, and strength in the knowledge that you have the power to shape your future. May you find your own river of peace, and may it guide you toward a future filled with resilience, compassion, wisdom, and love.

With loving kindness,

Heather Stang

REFERENCES

Every effort has been made to trace all copyright holders. Any omissions will be included in future editions if the publisher is notified.

Page 13: 1. Harris, D. L., *Counting Our Losses: Reflecting on Change, Loss, and Transition in Everyday Life* (Routledge, 2011); Harris, D. L. (ed.), *Non-death Loss and Grief: Context and Clinical Implications* (Routledge, 2020).

Page 16: 2. Parkes, C. M., "Psycho-social transitions: A field for study." *Social Science & Medicine, 5*(2), 101–115 (1971); Janoff-Bulman, R., *Shattered Assumptions: Towards a New Psychology of Trauma* (Free Press, 1992); Doka, K. J., "Disenfranchised grief and non-death losses" in *Non-death Loss and Grief*, pp. 25–35 (Routledge, 2019).

Page 27: 3. Doka, K. J., & Martin, T. L., *Grieving Beyond Gender: Understanding the Ways Men and Women Mourn* (Routledge, 2011).

Page 33: 4. Fenton, L. W., personal communication, 2024.

Page 34: 5. Rando, T. A., "Anticipatory Grief: The Term is a Misnomer but the Phenomenon Exists," *Journal of Palliative Care, 4*(1–2), 70–73 (1988).

Page 34: 6. Podcast: *Take Note: Dr. Tashel Bordere on Suffocated Grief* by Lindsey Whissel Fenton, WPSU, July 17, 2020 (https://radio.wpsu.org/education/2020-07-17/take-note-dr-tashel-bordere-on-suffocated-grief); Bordere, T., "Disenfranchisement and Ambiguity in the Face of Loss: The Suffocated Grief of Sexual Assault Survivors." *Family Relations, 66*: 29–45 (2017).

Page 36: 7. Boss, P., "Ambiguous Loss: Living with Frozen Grief." *Harvard Mental Health Letter, 16*(5) (1999).

Page 36: 8. Schultz, C. L., & Harris, D. L., "Giving voice to nonfinite loss and grief in bereavement" in *Grief and Bereavement in Contemporary Society*, pp. 235–245. (Routledge, 2011).

Page 36: 9. Bruce, E. J., & Schultz, C. L., *Nonfinite Loss and Grief: A Psychoeducational Approach* (Paul H Brookes Publishing, 2001).

Page 44: 10. Stroebe, M., & Schut, M. S. H., "The dual process model of coping with bereavement: Rationale and description." *Death Studies, 23*(3), 197–224 (1999).

Page 51: 11. Harris, D. L., "Midlife children caring for their aging parents" in *Non-Death Loss and Grief,* pp. 180–191 (Routledge, 2019).

Page 61: 12. Kabat-Zinn, J., *Full Catastrophe Living*, revised edition (Hachette UK, 2013).

Page 82: 13. Lichtenthal, W. G., & Cruess, D. G., "Effects of directed written disclosure on grief and distress symptoms among bereaved individuals." *Death Studies, 34*(6), 475–499 (2010).

Page 82: 14. Neimeyer, R. A. (ed.), *New Techniques of Grief Therapy: Bereavement and Beyond* (Routledge, 2021).

Page 91: 15. Doka, K. J., "Therapeutic ritual" in *Techniques of Grief Therapy*, pp. 341–343 (Routledge, 2012).

Page 111: 16. Worden, J. W., *Grief Counseling and Grief Therapy: A Handbook for the Mental Health Practitioner* (Springer Publishing Company, 2018).

FURTHER READING

Bancroft, L., & Patrissi, J. A. C., *Should I Stay or Should I Go?: A Guide to Knowing if Your Relationship Can—and Should—Be Saved* (Penguin Publishing Group, 2011)

Bauer-Wu, S., *Leaves Falling Gently: Living Fully with Serious & Life-Limiting Illness through Mindfulness, Compassion & Connectedness* (New Harbinger, 2011).

Bonanno, G. A., *The Other Side of Sadness: What the New Science of Bereavement Tells Us About Life After Loss* (Basic Books, 2009)

Boss, P., Ambiguous Loss: *Learning to Live with Unresolved Grief* (Harvard University Press, 2000)

Brach, T., *Radical Compassion: Learning to Love Yourself and Your World with the Practice of RAIN* (Penguin Publishing Group, 2019)

Calhoun, L. G., and Tedeschi, R. G., *Handbook of Posttraumatic Growth: Research and Practice* (Lawrence Erlbaum Associates, 2006)

Faulds, D., *Go In and In: Poems from the Heart of Yoga* (Peaceable Kingdom Books, 2002)

Goldberg, N., *Writing Down the Bones: Freeing the Writer Within* (Shambhala, 2005)

Levine, S., *Unattended Sorrow: Recovering from Loss and Reviving the Heart* (Rodale, 2005)

Mace, N. L., & Rabins, P. V. *The 36-Hour day: A Family Guide to Caring for People Who Have Alzheimer Disease, Other Dementias, and Memory Loss* (Johns Hopkins University Press, 2021)

Neff, K., *Self-Compassion: The Proven Power of Being Kind to Yourself* (William Morrow, 2011)

O'Connor, M. F., *The Grieving Brain: The Surprising Science of How We Learn from Love and Loss* (HarperOne, 2023)

Stang, H., *From Grief to Peace* (CICO Books, 2021)

Stang, H., *Living with Grief: Mindful Meditations and Self-care Strategies for Navigating Loss* (CICO Books, 2023)

Treleaven, D. A., *Trauma-Sensitive Mindfulness: Practices for Safe and Transformative Healing* (Norton, 2018)

RESOURCES

These resources can help you connect with a grief professional or support group.

Awaken Grief Support with Heather Stang heatherstang.com

Heather's Meditations on Insight Timer App insighttimer.com/heatherstang

US

Phoenix Rising School of Yoga Therapy Practitioner Directory pryt.com

Association of Death Education & Counseling adec.org

National Hospice and Palliative Care Organization caringinfo.org

National Alliance for Children's Grief nacg.org

American Association of Suicidology suicidology.org

988 Suicide & Crisis Lifeline Call or text 988; see also 988.lifeline.org

Open to Hope: Finding Hope After Loss opentohope.com

UK

The Samaritans samaritans.org / 116 123

CRUSE Bereavement Care cruse.org.uk and crusescotland.org.uk

USEFUL WEBSITES

Access mindfulness teachings through articles, podcasts, and events.

Insight Meditation Community of Washington, DC imcw.org

Deer Park Monastery deerparkmonastery.org

Pema Chödrön Foundation pemachodronfoundation.org

Be Mindful bemindful.co.uk

RETREAT CENTERS

Learn more about mindfulness, find a sangha, or schedule a retreat.

Shambhala (International Directory) shambhala.org

Spirit Rock Meditation Center spiritrock.org

Insight Meditation Society dharma.org

Kripalu Center For Yoga & Health kripalu.org

Omega Institute eomega.org

INDEX

ACKNOWLEDGMENTS

While my name may be the only one on the cover, everyone below deserves a byline. This book required me to navigate my own obstacles in writing, and these people helped light my way.

This book would not be the same without the stories shared by my clients, whose experiences have grounded the theories in practice. Their courage to open up and share their journeys through grief and healing provided invaluable insights and real-world applications for the concepts discussed in these pages. While they remain nameless to protect their confidentiality, their impact on this work is profound and deeply appreciated.

A deep bow of gratitude to Darcy Harris for her mission to ease suffering by acknowledging the losses that often go unacknowledged. Your mentoring, friendship, and model of true compassion and care are as cherished as a perfect shell on a pristine beach.

Lindsey Whissel Fenton, my cauldron sister and big spoon, your passionate advocacy for grieving persons, your ability to wordsmith even the most complex concepts, and your social media wizardry are invaluable.

My cherished colleagues Patti Anewalt, Claudia Coenen, Terri Daniel, Ken Doka, and Jason Wendroff-Rawnicki, your valuable feedback and professional insights ensured this book is both heart-centered and grounded in best practices. Your contributions shaped this work and my heart in ways words cannot fully express.

Phoenix Rising Yoga Therapy, created by Michael Lee and taught to me by him and the late Karen Hasskarl, is the philosophical throughline of everything I do. My love of mindfulness and meditation is credited to Jonathan Foust of the Insight Meditation Community of Washington. And I owe so much to Dana Cable and Terry Martin, my beloved thanatology professors at Hood College and both now deceased. I know you would both be on board with this new season in our field of grief and loss.

A special thanks to my publisher Carmel Edmonds and my editor Kristine Pidkameny, who championed this book. Your belief in this project and your guidance have been instrumental in bringing this book to life. Even though I moved as slow as a sloth at times, you have both been so patient.

Because community and food matter, the staff at Amani Brewing in Martinsburg, West Virginia, deserve a special mention. Thank you for allowing me to use your space as an office away from home, and for serving up delicious beverages, hummus, and pizza with a smile. Your kindness and hospitality were a crucial part of this book's journey.

I am grateful to my mother for bringing me into this world and gifting me with the best coffee machine a home-based writer could ever want. I am also thankful for my pupper Aerial, who keeps me moving and showers me with unconditional love. And finally, to Lisa Campbell and Karen Finneyfrock, for your friendship, wisdom, and support.